LIBERATING THE
BRIDE OF
CHRIST

*Loose Yourself . . . O Captive
Daughter of Zion*

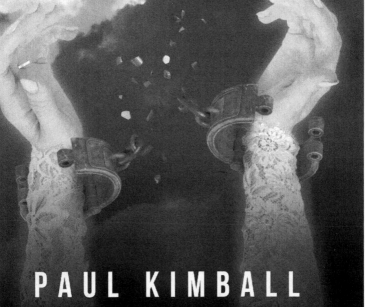

PAUL KIMBALL

Liberating the Bride of Christ:
Loose Yourself . . . O Captive Daughter of Zion

Copyright @ 2021 by Paul Kimball
ISBN: 978-1-949297-42-3
LCCN: 2021900375

Unless otherwise noted, all scriptures are from the KING JAMES VERSION, public domain.

Throughout this book, since I am quoting the King James Version of the Bible, I will use the singular "he/him" to refer to both the masculine and feminine "mankind."

There is no attempt to distinguish between male and female gender in this book, as my intent is purely to address those who are in Christ where gender is not relevant as the world knows it.

Scripture quotations marked (NKJV) are taken from the NEW KING JAMES VERSION®. Copyright© 1982 by Thomas Nelson, Inc. Used by permission. All rights reserved.

Address all personal correspondence to:

Paul Kimball
Email: *trimthelamps@gmail.com*

Individuals and church groups may order books from Pastor Paul Kimball directly, or from the publisher. Retailers and wholesalers should order from our distributors. Refer to the Deeper Revelation Books website for distribution information, as well as an online catalog of all our books.

Cover design and layout: Michael McDonald
artfx2@gmail.com

Published by:

Deeper Revelation Books
Revealing "the deep things of God" (1 Cor. 2:10)
P.O. Box 4260
Cleveland, TN 37320
423-478-2843
Website: *www.deeperrevelationbooks.org*
Email: *info@deeperrevelationbooks.org*

Deeper Revelation Books assists Christian authors in publishing and distributing their books. Final responsibility for design, content, permissions, editorial accuracy, and doctrinal views, either expressed or implied, belongs to the author.

DEDICATION

This book is dedicated to all those that the Holy Spirit has impregnated with an expectation and a hope that in this generation of the Church of the Lord Jesus Christ we will shake ourselves from the dust, arise, and sit down.

Isaiah 52:2 "Shake yourself from the dust, arise; Sit down, O Jerusalem! Loose yourself from the bonds of your neck, O captive daughter of Zion!" (NKJV)

Keep believing!

Acknowledgements

I am so thankful for the labor of love that my wife Rochelle has given in support of God's calling and also this writing. She slowly coaxed me to write with passion. She has been a faithful friend whose feedback I trust.

I am also thankful for Kelsey, Arlene, and Tyler, who each freely offered their feedback in a manner that impacted the writing of this book. Lastly (but by no means least), I want to thank Beverly, who labored in editing and dispensing constructive feedback which immensely improved the readability of this book.

I am also thankful for all the pastors that have, with the Holy Spirit, formed me into a man. And I would particularly like to thank Pastor Raffoul Najem for giving me opportunity to move into things ordained. He was answered prayer!

TABLE OF CONTENTS

INTRODUCTION
UNITY? OR DISUNITY?

It all started in the fall of 2016. This was when I began to see the body of Christ in a different light and to understand the calling of God on my life with more clarity. I became involved in a work that was started by the Holy Ghost who brought it to a place of revealing by the body of Christ.

I became aware of a small-town pastor that struggled to make ends meet and had come to a place where he could no longer continue in the house that he had rented for years. His wife had suffered a major stroke the year before; the new medical expenses, coupled with the modest pay of his daytime job, had brought him to a place of real financial trouble.

Throughout 2015, the Lord began to move pieces into place, preparing a truly glorious manifestation of His love and provision. First, a man sold him a relatively new mobile home for a few hundred dollars. Then, someone sold him several acres of land on a handshake with no interest and a pay-as-you-can payment plan. Next, the Lord provided a new concrete foundation, and after a few months, the mobile home was moved to the parcel of land and set up on the foundation.

This was in late spring of 2016, and from then until mid-September, I waited for some sign that he was moving. We had spoken several times about his situation, and I was aware that the first of November was a drop-dead date for him to be out of his rental property.

Finally, I approached him and said, "If there is anything I can do to help you prepare the new place, I want to help." He suggested that we go to the homestead and take a look. When I saw the mobile home sitting on its new foundation, I was not filled with joy or delight. Even though it was relatively new, the house did not appear to be in good shape. The doors hung, badly damaged, in their place, and there was no skirting to be seen. The threshold was forty-plus inches above grade, which meant a long and complicated ramp would need to be built to allow his wife to live in that mobile home.

We went inside, and my heart sank further. The floors were spongy and soft and rotted through in a number of places. The ceilings were dirty, and some walls were moldy. Sheetrock was falling off the studs in places, and the water pipes were all cracked. Everywhere I looked, there was work, a lot of work! I knew from experience that what I was looking at was much more than I could ever do alone. I also knew that the money needed to do this work was much more than I had to give.

However, once again, the Lord had provided for my friend, this time in the form of three-quarter-inch plywood flooring. There was enough flooring to cover the whole floor of the mobile home. Trying not to think about all the other things that would have to be addressed and knowing this pastor friend had no money for future supplies, I didn't have the heart to say anything, other than I would try to get the floor put down. The next day I gathered my tools and started the work.

After the floor was finished, I was constrained by the Lord to keep going. As time went on, I became aware of what the Lord was doing. My friend's spirit was broken; he seemed numb, a man with no hope. He had passed through an extended season of testing, and now the Lord purposed to heal him. Though work continued on, this hope had not yet taken hold in him.

This story is long and beautiful, but here is the part I want to get to. After a month of largely solo work for me, something began to change.

First, two brethren from the church body where I attended saw my labor and asked if they could help. A few weeks later, the wives of these men, as well as my own wife, asked if they could come and help with whatever we gave them to do. Then more brethren came forward. They offered to paint, to clean walls, bathroom, and windows, and even to cover the rental of a port-a-potty.

More and more volunteers came forward, not just from our congregation. Others joined from his own church body, from a congregation in the next town over, and from the town on the other side of that one. One Saturday, I took note that there were five congregations represented, all with one thing in common. With one heart, they all wanted to bless this pastor no matter what we gave them to do.

We labored as one. In the wind and the freezing rain, in snow and in heat, we worked. Some worked after their day job, some before their day job, and some on the weekends and holidays. Pastors washed walls, and elders painted them. A lieutenant colonel did material runs. Everyone paid a cost, and nobody complained at all. As the months passed, my friend's landlord was merciful, allowing the drop-dead move date to slip one month at a time.

The Lord used these people, these brethren, in this ministry to my pastor friend. As it was taking place, He opened my eyes to see His value of this labor of love we were doing. Each individual's labor was delightful to Him. He never checked to see their doctrinal position on the issues of the day; neither did He check to make sure they belonged to an approved denomination. My eyes were opened to see that the body of Christ is never according to denomination or organization and is not determined by doctrine alone. Rather, it is always seen in the labor of love that comes out of the heart of those that know Him. This love is unselfish, without desire for glory and not needing to rule. It is demonstrated through the redeemed of the Lord, loving as they had been taught.

During the entire four-month period, I never saw strife or competition, and the atmosphere was never unholy. All the things done for this pastor, and for me, were a revelation of the heart of the Lord God. He revealed the power of that love to me in this. One day we worked into the evening, mixing and pouring enough cement to fill fifty sauna tubes. We worked until our strength failed us. When we finished the last hole, utterly exhausted, we lifted our hands as one man and thanked the Lord for giving us the grace to do what we had done.

And from that very night, I saw hope revived in my friend.

Right before Christmas, he moved into a totally rebuilt mobile home, a miraculous provision of the Lord. I rested with my own very great reward. I had seen the body of Christ like never before!

After we finished the restoration of my friend's mobile home, the Holy Spirit continued to work on me. For many, many months I could not speak about what had happened without tears beginning to flow. My heart felt tender and broken, and I was continually in consideration of what I had seen and experienced. I began to consider how it could be possible to have experienced such a working of the Holy Ghost in me and yet have no place in the body of Christ opened where I could serve my brethren as a minister of the Word, a vocation to which I was called.

From early on in my salvation experience, the Holy Spirit had called me to a place of preaching the Word of God. I was now about thirty-five years in the faith, and from the very beginning, the Lord had brought me by way of consecration and prayer. Also, He had tested and proved me continually over those years, and I was increasingly aware of His strength in me. I valued this internal work of the Holy Ghost, and for many years had desired someone to mentor and make room for the grace that was on me. I had waited quietly so many years for someone to draw on this substance. Sadly, nobody drew on it; no one made room for it.

I knew the substance of this work of the Holy Spirit was more excellent than gold, and the sole purpose of this grace was for the perfecting of the saints. All around me, I saw the struggles of brethren in Christ. However, even though there was something powerful fermenting inside of me, and I felt full of the life of God, I had no place to speak. My wife was the only one who seemed to believe in the grace that was on me. I am so thankful for her. And I am so thankful for the labor and the spending that took place in that mobile home project. The Lord used it to confirm His intent in me.

So, through all of this contemplation, combined with what I had just experienced, I began to see that we, the Church, need to change. This is what I perceived: the disciples had three and a half years with the Lord Jesus, and they turned the world upside down. I had thirty-five years of walking with the Lord, and no doors opened.

It was out of the question to think the Holy Ghost had failed so greatly. My heart was hurt; it felt like I was robbed, or rather that the Lord Jesus Himself had been robbed. It seemed my life was passing by without having fruit to give to the Lord that spoke of His great grace that consumed me. I had no place to put these feelings and thoughts except at the feet of Jesus. Not until the Lord caused me to look back and consider ancient Babylon, did I begin to understand.

It feels like this book should be about the glory of this present Church and how we have become a splendid Bride, full of grandeur. Solomon's temple, with its gold, silver, and precious stones, declared the intended glory of this Church and this Bride—but oh, so dimly. We will look at this glorious purpose that our heavenly Father determined for the Church, using a third-person perspective, but will then begin to look forward through the generations that followed. From Jesus and the early Church, to the Azusa Street Revival, we will consider the progress of our heavenly Father's plan. However, when we come to our current Church age, we have to look back and consider a particular time in Israel's history— the captivity of Babylon. This exposes the age-old struggle of *all* God's people to give Him the one thing that He has always desired—love.

The intent of this book is to cause us to consider this insight from the Holy Ghost: Babylon is a type of religion, and religion is deadly. We need to also acknowledge that our present generation is one that is already captive to the spirit of Babylon. Now is a time to survey, as I did, where the body of Christ is. Why was I more broken by what I experienced, working shoulder to shoulder with those that I had never seen before, than I was by all the thousands of church services and sermons without number? I mean, I was unbelievably impacted by what I experienced!

Because of the need to consider and evaluate, I would like us to consider several questions. Do we know what being spiritually mature looks like? Do we honor titles more than the life of God that is wrought in the spiritually mature? Do we require honor for our title rather than honor for the reality of Christ that the Holy Spirit has fashioned in us? What has happened to the gifts of the Holy Spirit? How is it possible that most Holy Spirit-filled believers do not know or manifest the giftings of the Holy Spirit as part of a healthy congregation? Why do many worship services not reveal a celebration, adoration, and a victory that speaks to a great salvation?

I pray that you would grant me grace in this attempt at writing and that we may consider together where we are and how we go forward.

CHAPTER 1

OUR HEAVENLY FATHER'S PERFECT GIFT

For the first few years that my wife and I were married, things were very tight financially. However, I was so in love with her and so desiring to bless her, that I would save up (from the little I had) and buy her little pieces of jewelry: a necklace, a ring, earrings, etc. She loved gold jewelry; so, knowing she had grown up with little, it became an easy way to bless her with something she truly enjoyed, and, at the same time, communicate that I was madly in love with her. When it came time to pick up the gift at the jewelers, I could barely contain myself. Usually it was quite a struggle to keep my secret until I had given her the gift and had seen the joy on her face.

Most of us can relate to this experience in one way or another, but have we considered how the pulse of our heavenly Father races when He considers the gift that He has purposed to give to His Son Jesus Christ? I don't mean to reduce the Father of all creation to my level, but I was made in His image.[2] How do we know if this desire to bless those that we love wasn't created in us to reflect His own passion for His beloved Son[3] and for all those that believe in His Son?[4] Even as my anticipation mounted to a level where I could barely contain myself after I had set my heart to give my wife a special gift, surely it is the same for our heavenly Father, only so, so much greater.

Why is His anticipation and desire so much greater than mine? It's because our heavenly Father's heart is pure, His honor is pure, and His knowledge is complete.[5] He knows the supreme sacrifice of His Son Jesus like no one else does. He esteems the sacrifice of Jesus so much that His heart is overwhelmed with the desire to honor and bless Him. Nothing but the best. Only the perfect! [6] Only the strong! Only the pure![7] What could He possibly give to His Son that would be a worthy gift?

Our heavenly Father decreed that He would make a people to stand at the side of His Son through all eternity. Perhaps this thought was in our Father's heart: "This people will be called the body of Christ; they will reveal all of my Son's heart and mind." This people would be a beautiful and glorious people, beyond any comparison.[8] Theirs would be a beauty that is only found in the very nature of God, and they would manifest all of His character. He would make for His Son Jesus a Bride that would be a glorious helpmate[9] for all eternity!

When God made man in His image, He had His Son's gift in mind. Where the Bible said "male and female created He them,"[10] He had put this gift in motion. Was He only speaking forth the creation of gender? In this we see the incredible wisdom of our God. The natural beauty of a woman only prophesies to the glory of God's people. Some women have a very apparent beauty, and others do not. So, though some have a particular physical glory and others do not, all, male and female, have the potential through Jesus to reveal a glory in this realm and the next that is much, much greater. This is a glory that radiates out of the heart and the spirit of one who is rescued from the power of darkness by the Lord Jesus Christ and transformed by the working of the Holy Spirit. This is the glory that belongs to the redeemed of the Lord, the heavenly Bride of Christ.

The people that were predestined to be joined to the Lord Jesus Christ and to stand at His side would have to show forth this glory of the redeemed. This is a beauty that only comes from honest interactions with the Word of Truth and the bountiful supply of the Holy Ghost.[11] The washing of the water by the Word slowly eliminates everything that is corrupt and defiling, while the renewing of the Holy Ghost causes the glory of the nature of God Himself to begin to shine forth.[12] This Bride, which is made up of many members, would have to be without blemish and without fault, just men made perfect. How could a fallen creation such as man ever come to this place of perfection? This people would have to pass from the confines of a temporal existence into the glorious limitlessness of the life of our God. Our heavenly Father knew that to bring such a people out of the darkness of this present world into the glory of His own living and to present that people unto His beloved Son would be an exceedingly great miracle!

Only He could foresee the way that each individual member of that great holy people would have to come. They would have to come by fire so that everything that could be burnt up would be burnt up. Every motive would be examined, and every way would be cleansed. Sadly, He knew that many would not love Him enough, and because of this, they would not have the strength or power to make this journey.[13] However, all those people who overcame would be incredibly fashioned, truly unmovable, and miraculously faithful. God Almighty would make a people forged in the fire and individually fashioned into the exactness of what God foreknew. Hallelujah!

So, the wisdom of God stood at the end of time, and He considered the perfectness of His own great plan. He

21

saw every faultless feature, every ability, and every attribute of each one of this holy people and understood how greatly they would please His Holy Son. He considered each particular member that would make up this great people and determined that, by the power of His grace, He would save to the uttermost every single member of this glorious Bride.

You might ask, if the Lord God made a people, wouldn't they be perfect already? Why should there be all this consideration and all this forethought over a perfection that He could just make? It was because the Lord resolved to make man in His image, and, being in His image, man would have a will. He would not force men to love, but rather, they would choose to love.[14] Each member of the Bride would choose to obey, choose to yield, and choose to walk as a child before His presence.[15] They would each choose to lay down their life so others could live. Our eternal, wise Father would literally cause the heart of His Son Jesus to be formed in each and every member that makes up this precious Bride. All of this He considered before the world began! So, He stood at the beginning of time and created man; as Genesis 5:2 tells us, "Male and female created He them."

God knew because man was made from the dust of the earth and had not yet partaken of the divine nature of God, he would be able to be tempted to disobey. He saw that mankind would yield to temptation, fall into sin and darkness, and be powerless to help themselves. But, in due time, Almighty God Himself would send forth an answer. He would send the Word of God Himself to put on flesh and walk as a man in the person of Jesus Christ.[16] As a man, and with His own life, Jesus would defeat the sentence of death and free a people from their dark bondages.[17] Jesus would become the way of escape and the forgiver of all the debts of sin for every single soul that turned to Him.

The Lord God, from the beginning, saw that His Son Jesus would lay down His life to purchase this great and innumerable people.[18] Whoever believed in Him would receive His Holy Spirit. This Holy Spirit would live in them, teach them, and empower them to become pure in spirit and soul.

This would not be a theoretical victory, with no manifested triumph. A fallen man, even Adam as he was first made, could not possibly walk the path that must be walked. It was the Holy Spirit dwelling in each and every member of the body of Christ who would empower the redeemed and give them everything they would need to make this great journey. Step by step, obedience by obedience, the Holy Ghost would bring forth hope in the midst of a hopeless world.[19] Wells of hope! Springs of hope! The hope of our heavenly Father Himself. His Son would have a Bride!!

How precious is this Bride to God? How can we possibly know, if there has never been anything like her? However, there is a way to get an idea of her value. Let's consider one of the other scriptural names for this same holy people: a holy temple.

Scripture refers to the temple of Israel as the dwelling place of God; it's where His presence would remain. Individually, we are considered to be the temple of the Holy Ghost because when we repent from our dead works, come under the precious blood of our Savior, and are filled with the Holy Ghost, it is God Himself that takes up residence in us.[20] Also, collectively, we who believe and obey are built into a holy edifice, a holy temple,[21] where God Himself will dwell throughout eternity. So, we, the Church, have many scriptural descriptions, but it is the same people that will make up the Bride as will make up the temple!!

23

By looking at the temples of Israel, we can begin to understand the significance of the living and eternal God dwelling in the midst of a people. None of the former temples exactly describe what we will be or look like throughout eternity, but they do foreshadow the Church of the living God. By foreshadowing, I mean to speak to a thing without clarity or exactness. The accounts of the temples, whether the tent of meeting, Solomon's temple, or the temple that Ezekiel saw, speak to aspects of our life of worship and our salvation. Each one is filled with types and symbols that speak to the richness of God's goodness, His wisdom, and His presence among His people.[22]

For the sake of gleaning insight into how greatly our heavenly Father esteems the people that love His Son Jesus, those whom He will present as a Bride to His Son, let's look at the account of Solomon's temple. David, the king, had a great desire to honor God. He personally knew Him as Deliverer, Provider, Protector, Judge, and Merciful Savior. His heart was very tender toward his God. The king began to set aside materials for this great work.

King David set aside one hundred thousand talents of gold and one million talents of silver to build a house for God (today's combined value of that gold and silver is, conservatively, fifty-six billion dollars). Then, because his longing over this vision was so great, he gave an additional three thousand talents in gold and seven thousand talents of pure silver out of his own money. Six hundred talents of gold were to be used in the Holiest of Holies itself (this amount of gold is approximately forty-five thousand pounds of gold).[23] What an incredible thing! It's incredible because the holiest of holies represents the human spirit as found in a disciple of Christ,[24] and the gold represents the divine nature of our God. We are to be so transformed that all God sees in us is Himself! Hallelujah! Moving on, the walls, ceilings, beams, and doors of the temple were also coated in pure gold. This is a temple whose plan came from God himself. So, what exactly was He saying?

This passage speaks to the incredible measure of the nature and the character of our Lord God, as well as the great redemptive work (seen in the vast amount of silver) that is found in the workmanship of the temple of the living God. I believe with all of my heart that this is what our heavenly Father saw when He looked upon the finished work of our redemption.

God Himself is the only one that could possibly do this work and bring forth such a glorious creation. Only His mind could see such a spectacle before it even began. Only His faith could possibly prevail over all the darkness and all the sin and bring this great work to completion. Finally, only the love of God could endure all things, bear all things, believe all things, hope all things[25]—and only He would suffer all things.

God the Father, God the Son, and God the Holy Ghost undertook as one to bring forth a people—and what a people they would be.[26] They are the Bride of the Lord Jesus Christ, the Church of the living God. Hallelujah!

CHAPTER 2

A GLORIOUS BEGINNING

We leave the beginning and journey on through time, from the creation of man until the coming of the Lord Jesus Christ. During that span of time, the world saw the fall of mankind into a darkened state, where people lived with no consideration of God. The darkness in men's hearts became so dark and filled with violence that the heart of God was actually grieved; He was sorry He made man.[27] And so, He determined to start over.

There was a man called Noah living in that time, and he "found grace in the eyes of the Lord."[28] Genesis 6:9 says that he was "a just man and perfect in his generations, and Noah walked with God." The Lord spoke to him and instructed him to build an ark, a great boat, which would not only carry Noah's immediate family, but also two of every living kind of animal. Then the Lord God sent a great flood, and it covered the earth, destroying all living creatures. After the flood waters abated, and as He had decreed, the Lord started over again with Noah's family, just eight souls. From these eight souls, He brought forth all of humanity, and He commanded them to spread over the earth.

From the lineage of Noah came the man Abram, and the Lord commanded him to leave his country and his family and go to a land that He would show him. The man Abram went forth, stopping here and there to build altars and to worship. After the last of his family (Lot, Abram's nephew), was separated from him, God came to Abram and told him to look as far as he could to the north, the south, the east, and the west. The Lord said He would give all that land to him and to his seed as an inheritance forever.[29]

This was a time in Abram's life where God chose to institute a covenant with him. The Lord God promised Abram a child in his old age and said that no longer was his name to be Abram, but Abraham, a father of nations. The Lord said that Abraham's descendants would be as the dust of the earth in number. Sure enough, out of Abraham and Sarah came the nation that was to be called Israel. Israel became a people without a country, living for four hundred years[30] in the midst of Egypt where they began to be persecuted and abused.

At the time foreseen, the Lord God of Abraham brought the Israelites out of Egypt with a mighty outstretched hand. His desire for Israel was holiness; they would love and serve Him only. Moses led the children of Israel out of Egypt, commissioned by God to bring them into the promised land of Canaan. This was only an eight-day journey, but it would take the Israelites forty years to get there because of their unbelief and grumbling.

For the next 1,500 years, the Israelites journeyed in the land of Canaan. Victors they were and victims, righteousness they did and evil, revivals they had and apostasies. They did it all and experienced it all, but eventually there was silence. Their God and their deliverer had been hurt too many times by His own people. Now He would shut His prophets' mouths and wait. The

Father of Israel would wait until the appointed time, the time of the promise of His own beloved Son!

Most are familiar with the birth of Jesus Christ, the Messiah, so, let's move on until the beginning of the earthly ministry of our Savior. When Jesus, the Son of God, turned thirty years of age, He began to preach. His was a message of repentance and a message of hope.[31] This message of Christ was not focused on the revival of a nation that had failed in their vows to God. Rather, He proclaimed deliverance and healing, forgiveness of sins, and the releasing of those who were bound. This was a gospel of mercy and not judgement, a message of freedom from oppression, and the possibility of a right response to the Spirit of God.[32] He would, by Himself, establish a kingdom whose foundation was His own right response to the will of His heavenly Father, thereby fulfilling the law and the prophets.

With demonstrations of power and authority, the Lord Jesus walked the roads of Judea for three and a half years. He was filled with grace and truth[33] and manifested the exact nature and character of the eternal God in all He said and did.[34] No sinner was rejected, no sick was turned away, nor any that were possessed; He healed them all. Jesus uttered a command in one place, and miles away the devils obeyed Him. Jesus was as powerful to heal and to deliver at a distance as when he actually laid hands on someone. He didn't ask the Father to do a healing, but rather He exercised the authority His heavenly Father had given Him. Jesus also confronted the religious sector, the Scribes and the Pharisees, with the grace and truth of one who had yielded His whole being subject to the will of His Father. There was not an ounce of hypocrisy in the life or the doctrine of Jesus Christ.

As Lord, he manifested dominion over all things. But He was also Master, and as such, He called certain men to walk with Him and become His disciples. These men were not particularly special or unique. Some were fishermen (small businessmen), and one was a tax collector. They were not men of learning or culture, not big fish in the Jewish culture; in contrast, they came from the small pond of Galilee. Galileans were known for not being overly consumed with the legalities of Jewish law,[35] and, presumably, this meant that His disciples were more open to hear the doctrine of their new Master.

For three and a half years, Jesus walked among these twelve, keeping them close to Himself and imparting to them the knowledge and wisdom that came directly from His Father in heaven. This knowledge was pure because it sprang forth out of His relationship with His heavenly Father. It was not biased by the traditions of the Jews or colored by the ambitions of an earthly heart. It was not distorted by pride or arranged to cover insecurities. This was a knowledge and a wisdom that came forth out of a pure vessel, a vessel that had been set apart for one use and one use only: to do the will of the Father.[36]

When Jesus forgave the woman caught in adultery, He was teaching the twelve to show mercy. In speaking to Peter, "Get behind Me, Satan! You are an offense to Me, for you are not mindful of the things of God, but the things of man,"[37] He imparted a lesson of great importance, to always distinguish between your spirit and soul. With just a word, He cast the devil out of a child that had been possessed a long time. This was moments after His disciples had failed to cast the same devil out. Jesus used that occasion to give the disciples a great key: "However, this kind does not go out except by prayer and fasting."[38] When He got up in the middle of the night and went into the mountains to pray, He gave them another precious key: at whatever the cost, a minister must have time apart with just the Father. A boat in the midst of the sea was the classroom where the Lord cautioned against hypocrisy when He said, "Beware of the leaven of the Pharisees, which is hypocrisy."[39]

The disciples saw the power of creation in the feeding of the five thousand, and the authority of the Son of God over nature in the calming of the seas and the walking on water. He instructed them to be subject to the civil authorities when He said, "Render to Caesar the things that are Caesar's, and to God the things that are God's."[40] For three and a half years, Jesus walked with the disciples, and, by example, taught them all things pertaining to the life of a Son.

When the time of instruction was done, and He hung crucified on the cross, the Master of all masters taught them the greatest lesson of all: "Greater love has no one than this, than to lay down one's life for his friends."[41] He had finished His course and had made the greatest hand-off that has ever been made. He had given His disciples all that He had and all that He was!

All of the Lord's earthly ministry laid the ground-work for the glorious beginning of the Church of the living God. If Jesus Christ had not manifested even one of the things that He did, or if He did not teach even one of the things that He did, the apostles would have become weak or vulnerable in that area in which they were not instructed. His life, however, was perfect, and His teachings were without fault and complete. So, as the Lord Jesus Christ prepared to ascend into heaven and take His seat at the right hand of God, His disciples were prepared and instructed for the ministry that lay before them. Still, upon His ascension, the Lord commanded His disciples to "Tarry in Jerusalem until you are endued with power from on high."[42]

As we read the Book of the Acts of the Apostles, it is impossible not to be moved by the events that Acts records. In the second chapter of Acts, we see 120 of the disciples gathered in an upper room, and the scripture says they were in "one accord."[43] All of the sudden, a tremendous spiritual happening took place. The Holy Ghost of God fell upon them, and the appearance of tongues of fire sat upon each. They didn't shed a pious tear and then go on their way unchanged, and they didn't sit quietly; rather, they began to make a commotion and a ruckus.

There was shouting and noise! The word spread like wildfire, and many people from the city quickly began to gather. When the people came, they saw the 120 disciples, who looked to be intoxicated. They heard much speaking, all at once, and to the amazement of the people that came, they heard these ragged, uneducated bunch of disciples proclaiming the glory of God in the native tongues of those that came. What had happened was not, as some of these observers thought, that these disciples had taken up drinking. Rather, the heavenly Father had poured out upon them the promised Holy Spirit!

This was the power that Jesus had commanded them to wait for.[44] As a group, none of them knew what would happen in the days to come, but at that moment they were indomitable. Their spirits were flushed with the power of God, and they were not ashamed at all. Peter saw the people gathering and did not hesitate. He stood up and began to preach the kingdom of heaven. There was no start time for that church service and no end time. Rather, it was just an opportunity that the Holy Ghost had opened up, and he began to preach. His message was simple, but the effect was tremendous; three thousand souls were added into the kingdom of God that day.

Therefore, in one day, the Church was born. The program of the early Church was simple, and it appears that their living was also simple. The scripture says, "They continued steadfastly in the apostles' doctrine and fellowship."[45] Here, "steadfastly" means to do something with intense effort despite difficulty. This Church had a common faith, and that appears to be the basis for their fellowship. However, it also showed a very practical example of living as a community because Acts 2:42 continues, "And in the breaking of bread, and in prayers."

You can see the beginning of a church body in this passage, with Christ Himself as the head. The Church was young, but the believers had one love and one purpose. The Holy Ghost had imparted something into them that set them on this course of simplicity. There was no church building, only the people of God and the presence of God—and it was enough. What was the fruit of this daily commitment to their newfound faith and to each other?

The scripture says that the fear of the Lord came upon every soul.[46] The apostles did many wonders and signs, and the Lord added to the Church daily such as should be saved. The whole atmosphere of Jerusalem was changing as people were added to the Church. Peter preached another time, and five thousand men were saved. Fear and awe filled the assemblies, and the Holy Ghost confirmed what was happening with many signs and wonders. What followed was a surge of fear in the religious leaders of the day.

These religious leaders began to persecute the church leaders: threatening Peter and John, beating the apostles, and killing Stephen and James. This did not hinder the disciples at all; neither was there a decrease of the presence of God in the midst of them. People were raised from the dead, the blind received their sight, and the lame were made to walk. Surely God was sanctified in the body of Christ; He had a people! Out of this atmosphere, the apostles and the brethren began to push outward, to all of Judea, and then into the Gentile countries. Concerning them the unbelieving Jewish leaders declared that they had "turned the world upside down."[47]

Such is the beginning of the Church!

CHAPTER 3

WHOOPS, WE MISSED THE HAND-OFF

We have now taken a glimpse into the life and ministry of the Lord Jesus Christ and how one of His main efforts as Master was to teach and train His disciples to walk in the same way that He walked. This was not done in a classroom setting, but rather on the dusty roads of Judea and on the stormy seas. The disciples were coupled to Him day and night, and they literally experienced the message He preached. His manner of living and teaching wrote something upon their hearts and their minds. There is no record of any of them straying from His tutelage all the days of their lives. He had successfully handed off to His disciples all that He knew and believed.

Miracles, signs, wonders, and many, many souls were added to the kingdom; all indications spoke that the Church was firmly established and growing as planned. But if we read more carefully, we see that there were also places of disagreements and schisms. Judaism was always present, trying to get believers to begin to observe ordinances and days that belonged to the Jews' old covenant.[48] In addition, the apostle Paul spoke this about false teachers: "Who concerning the truth have erred, saying that the resurrection is past already; and overthrow the faith of some."[49]

Sects also sprang up; this group said they belonged to this apostle, and that group professed allegiance to another.[50] The apostles continually battled against sin in the Church: carnality, immorality, greed, and all manner of unholy living.[51] Still, the faith of the apostles was strong, and they prevailed over all of these things by manifesting the authority of the kingdom of heaven given to them by the Lord Jesus Christ.

God didn't purpose that we live forever, and that was true for the apostles. They aged and began to die, one by one laying down their lives in martyrdom. As the voice of each one fell silent, the holy rebuke and the setting in order that they had brought to the Church also began to be silenced. The book of Joshua tells us, "Israel served the Lord all the days of Joshua, and all the days of the elders who outlived Joshua, who had known all the works of the Lord."[52] The book of Judges then records, "All that generation were gathered unto their fathers: and there arose another generation after them, which knew not the Lord, nor yet the works which He had done for Israel."[53] I believe this is exactly what happened with the early Church.

The first sermon I ever preached, which the Holy Spirit had impressed on me, was called "Third-Generation Pentecostalism." The first generation of a Pentecostal movement belonged to a people that lived what they believed. Their faith was strong, and they were acquainted with the suffering of the cross. They were persecuted for their belief and were lowly in spirit. Even if their doctrine was not perfect, God was with them because they feared and honored Him. That first generation saw many miracles and demonstrations of God's might. God added many souls to them because, frankly, their lives were consecrated.

I had a personal experience relating to this about forty years ago when I attended a regional camp meeting of the United Pentecostal Church. After the time of worship, the speaker got up and made his way to the pulpit. I still remember his white hair and his aged appearance. But as he took his place behind the podium and raised his hands, the glory of God fell upon the whole place. I do not remember a word that he spoke, but I cannot write this account without my eyes flooding with tears. I don't know anything about that man except what we experienced that evening. However, I believe out of that man of God's reverent and godly living, the Lord imparted the fear of the Lord to me, and I have never looked back. That man belonged to the "First-Generation Pentecostals."

The "Second-Generation Pentecostals" were good people, outwardly carrying on the example that was given to them. However, change came. Some change was by necessity as God had added many souls. Now the Church required more effort to keep those who had been given them versus reaching out to get more. Leaders directed more teachings at maturing the Christian than in reaching the lost. The biggest change came in the place of prayer. Their forefathers had spent many hours a day in prayer,[54] groaning under the need to bring forth fruit into the kingdom of heaven. Those hours of prayer diminished, which began to affect the strength of spirit, the focus of the heart, and the vision of these Second-Generation Pentecostals.

Lastly, the Spirit showed me the third generation of such a movement. Their forefathers were now dead, and in their place stood a people who were not familiar with the depths of the Spirit of God. Also, most were not acquainted with the pain and suffering frequently experienced in the working out of such a precious faith. The study of the Word of God can become more of a quest for knowledge and not a hunger for one's spiritual sustenance. Most importantly, because the flesh is at enmity with God, one's prayer life can further decay into a sometime thing. At that point, prayer becomes only when we need something, and the prevailing prayer—weeping and the faithful bearing of burdens in prayer—becomes scarce. I heard a preacher recently say, "We can lose the art of the tremble."[55] He spoke this concerning the need for all of us to experience the presence of God to such a degree that our goodness flees away, and His mercy and grace is what is left. We need to be close enough to tremble.

The Spirit had opened this up to me almost forty years ago, and it seems exactly like what I am seeing when I look back at the early Church. Absolutely nothing is more important for any generation than to impart to the next generation a love for the presence of God. Somewhere in that timeframe of the second-to-third generation from Christ, leaders of the Church began to teach from a place of knowledge and not from a place of revelation. Teachers began to instruct men with their lips and not with their spirit.[56] A generation arose that did not understand one of the most important things the Lord did for us was to rend the veil in two. The way into the holiest was opened for every single one of God's children. In the presence of the Lord, we will always find everything we need to continue from generation to generation. In spite of this, around 150 A.D., a generation arose that did not know the way to the throne of God.

From the glory of this first apostolic ministry, to the rise of the Roman Catholic Church, another era emerged. The era in which the excellent strength of our salvation was openly manifested to all transitioned to a period of spiritual darkness where truth was lost. Religious ritual and cruel enforcements of men took its place. To glean insight into the explanation of this incredible spiritual transformation that took place in just a few hundred years, let's look back at the nation of Israel, back to the time of Samuel.[57] I believe with all of my heart that our God made sure we could see every single thing in the scriptures so that we would be able to face the obstacles and challenges of this age.

CHAPTER 4

WE WANT A KING

I believe the center of salvation is grace. The secret of any disciple being full of grace is his place of individual fellowship with the Lord in the Spirit. No one can do anything eternal without the presence of the Lord. The problem is, all men have a carnal nature, and the carnal nature is not, nor ever will be, inclined to desire the presence of God or to be faithful or fervent toward Him. Inherently, every believer's carnal nature desires a buffer or a cushion between him and our Holy God. Whatever that buffer is, its purpose to the flesh is to weaken the effect of God's holiness and absorb the force of His presence so that we don't have to change.

Our desire for a spiritual buffer is first seen in Exodus when the children of Israel desired Moses to go up into the mount to meet with God and then come back and be the voice of God to them. When they saw the thundering and lightning and heard the trumpet of God, they actually removed themselves from the presence of God and stood afar off.[58]

The Israelites also revealed this same fleshly heart a little later when they approached Samuel the prophet and said, "Give us a king."[59] Israel's request displeased the prophet Samuel, who brought it to the Lord in prayer. The Lord God told Samuel to give them what they wanted as they were not rejecting Samuel, but Him.[60] God also told the prophet to speak very plainly to the children of Israel to make them understand what having a king was going to cost them. In every area of their living, they would pay a price for their wanting to be like other nations in this desire for a king.

God had determined to have a people that He could have a relationship with. He wanted to be their husband,[61] their protector,[62] their provider, and their judge. The Lord wanted to dwell in the midst of Israel and to have the land filled with rejoicing[63] and peace; however, He knew what would happen. The Lord God knew that having a king would result in more sin in the land of Israel, and sin could and would break that relationship.

True to form, when Joshua and the elders passed away, the children of Israel began to leave their appointed place of relationship with the Lord God and journey into unmistakable spiritual darkness. They began to lose their way and their place of relationship with God. As we peruse the scriptures, we can see this transformation take place with the nation of Israel during the time after Joshua. It's the exact same thing which began to happen in the early Church. When the apostles began to pass away, the sheer force of their spirit and the strength of their faith no longer influenced the early Church, and the Church began to lose its way also.

Why spend this chapter considering the desire of the Israelites to have a king, this buffer between them and God? Because this was a real desire of Israel's heart, and it's also a temptation for all those of the age of grace. Why? Because there is no new thing under the sun. We all have an earthly nature that fights to escape the accountability of God's calling. We also have to consider this desire because of who this nation of Israel is; they are a people that speaks to a greater time and a greater people. Their victories, their defeats, the things they won, and the things they lost all allude to us, the Church of the Lord Jesus Christ.[64]

Israel's request to have a king showed they had a heart that was ready for the re-emergence of Babylon (religion). It declared their heart was not really interested in walking with God and being accountable to Him in a one-on-one relationship. That same heart emerged once again after the time of the apostles. The majority of those that professed the name of the Lord showed themselves to be perfectly content to leave the study of Scripture, the perceptions of the times, and the interpretation of the individual requirements of righteousness to a mediator (a pastor or teacher or bishop) instead of walking with God in the Spirit. However, the Holy Spirit says to the Church, to every man, that there is given an accountability to deal with God, according to the truth that has been given to him. This is true no matter the people or the generation.[65]

So, for the same reason that Israel wanted a king, the Church that followed the generation of the apostles began to see the rise of structure and the rule of men in the Church and the resulting subordination of the vast majority of the redeemed. Titles mean authority, and if there was one thing that was very apparent in the time of Jesus Christ, men wanted to rule and exercise dominion. However, when there is a rise of men exercising dominion in the Church of the Living God, it causes a buffer and a cushion that shelters a generation of souls from the weight of God's holiness.

We'll look more at Babylon in the next chapters and consider how it prophesies to the time after the Azusa Street Revival. For now, I'll leave you with this thought: The desire to have a king is indicative of a lazy and adulterous heart, as is the contentment to spend one's whole spiritual life eating only what others provide instead of learning to take our place at the Lord's table. This is where the Spirit of God serves up eternal sustenance, and by eating this, we begin falling in love with the fullness of our God. The Lord Jesus purchased a place of intimate fellowship for every one of us with the laying down of His life.

A thousand times over, I am not opposed to the offices of the teacher or pastor. All of the present-day Church desperately needs these offices functioning in all the power and glory of the apostolic age. But these are very holy offices and must be filled with the substance of God that is found only in mature sons. Something unfortunately changed in the Church after the apostles died, and I feel like it is tied to the words of the apostles themselves: "But we will give ourselves continually to prayer and to the ministry of the word."[66]

It's like the law of gravity. If we draw close to the Lord and delight in Him through prayer, study of the Word of God, fasting, and obedience to the Holy Spirit, our hearts will be drawn ever closer to Him. We become full of faith and full of the Spirit and revelation. But if we leave those places of spiritual fellowship, our hearts will be drawn ever closer to this world and be filled with earthly reasonings and earthly desires. This was the path into the Dark Ages for the early Church.

CHAPTER 5

DARKNESS

For several generations, the light of the Church burned brightly. Then it began to dim; something had changed. What followed next was a journey into darkness, sometimes referred to as the "Dark Ages." It was here, for 1400 years or so, the Roman Catholic Church ruled in the world of religion. Then, in the early 1500s, men began to separate from Catholicism in what is now called the "Reformation." The doctrine that came forth in the early years of the Reformation laid the foundation of theology as was seen in the early 1900s.

This period of church history is not the example that we should look to pattern our living after. Periods of violence, persecution, immorality, and greed took place within the Roman Catholic Church throughout this time. The Church branded every new thought, anything not matching its position, as heresy, and excommunicated or killed the author of such thought.

Even though history presents the Dark Ages as a period without light, I am positive that's not the whole truth. In every generation God has had a remnant who fear His name and walk before Him as those that consider Him.[67] Someone is always praying, always asking his heavenly Father to bring His kingdom and establish it in a people. With all of my heart, I lift up a thank you for every unseen, faithful soul that, on his knees, laid the foundation for the Reformation. I offer thanksgiving also for everyone who called for truth when it was overshadowed by the perspectives of men, even when persecution followed.

CHAPTER 6

AZUSA STREET

In 1906, a revival of the Holy Spirit took place on Azusa Street in Los Angeles, California—and it shook the world. It seemed like it was the very beginning of something. But in fact, there had been a continual progression of truth since the days of Martin Luther and the beginning of the Reformation. It was, however, an intense re-emergence of the experience of the baptism of the Holy Spirit with much demonstration of the gifts of the Spirit in all those that gathered.[68]

People from all over the world heard the news of this great outpouring and came running. The revival touched so many souls who were healed, delivered, and filled with the Holy Ghost. When they left the Azusa Street Mission, they were full of fire and full of the witness of the Holy Spirit. Returning to wherever they came from, they began to manifest the glorious reality of the gospel of the Lord Jesus Christ as they had experienced it.[69] Many healing ministries sprang up, such as the ministries of John G. Lake and F. F. Bosworth.[70] Thousands of missionaries went forth over the whole earth, bringing this glorious experience to believers and unbelievers everywhere. One could think this was surely the last day, where the Lord Jesus Christ returns, and the Church exits gloriously. However, we must consider something else in that great event.

This was a very real and very glorious work of the Holy Spirit,[71] and so many people were instantly changed. However, the Lord had yet to reveal an even greater glory. How do I know that for sure? I know it because of the fact that many denominations came forth from this event: the Assemblies of God, the Church of God, the Church of God in Christ, the Pentecostal Holiness Church, and later the United Pentecostal Church. It's also because of this very reason that the outpouring on the Azusa Street Mission stopped. It was the bitter and heated disagreement over doctrine that caused the people of Azusa to splinter and many denominations to spring forth. It is almost impossible to believe that this incredible outpouring of the Holy Ghost ended because of an intense disagreement concerning whether a believer is sanctified before or after the baptism of the Holy Ghost. REALLY? The greater glory to yet be revealed is the unity in the Spirit, which did not come forth from Azusa Street. The Church of Jesus Christ was still a people divided.

It's good to look back and see these milestones of faith, but all of this only highlights the need for us to go on. We must understand that the Holy Ghost is surely working out this salvation, this great work of redemption over many generations, but the vision of God is still the same. Our heavenly Father will have a glorious Bride for the Lord Jesus Christ! It must also become our vision.

CHAPTER 7

THE ENLIGHTENED
CHURCH

I'm calling the people and the age that came forth out of the Azusa Street Revival "the enlightened Church." This is said a little tongue in cheek because I actually believe that was the beginning of a time of spiritual blindness. What I mean is this: the next one hundred years after Azusa is a period that has seen Spirit-filled revivals, the charismatic movement, great healing ministries, and the springing up of countless seminaries and Christian colleges, all apparently wonderful kingdom growth. However, it has also seen countless groups and splinter groups spring up, grace be cheapened, and faith wane. Pulpit after pulpit has fallen to adultery, homosexuality. The fear of the Lord is scarce, and when Christians do spend time together in fellowship, many times the focus is not on the Spirit of God. To hear it told, we are in such a time of spiritual plenty, recipients of such a great spiritual heritage; how can both reports be true? What is the truth about the state of the Church?

After the mobile home project, I had many questions that needed answers. Sure enough, as I sought the Lord, I began to get them. Some answers came through the Word, some came through prayer, and some came by dreams. It was in the early morning of July 29, 2016, that my wife had a very vivid dream:

> The setting appeared to be a very large, indoor swimming pool filled with a lot of people. They were playing and laughing, and everyone was having fun. I saw a very good friend there. Although it seemed I knew many of the people there, hers was the only face that stuck with me. She was in the water, so I walked to the edge of the pool and got into the water but immediately got out; I'm not sure why. However, my sense was that I wanted to help her. I resolved to get back into the pool, even though I sensed danger. As I went to get back into the water, I saw that most of the water had drained out of the pool, but all the people were still in the pool as if nothing was happening. As I continued getting back in the water, the rest of the water drained out. The emptying of the pool revealed huge worms, a foot in diameter and five or six feet long, filling its bottom. In spite of this, the people stayed in the pool as if nothing were wrong, as if nothing were happening. I could feel the worms under my feet; then, I woke up.

My wife ascertained that the worms were principalities and powers of darkness. As they enjoyed themselves in the pool, the people thought it was a time of peace, completely unaware of the presence of darkness. They were deceived into thinking that it was a time of calm, a time of pleasure, and a time to be merry. All the while, the worms beneath them were ready to consume them.

What I ascertained was that the water signifies a word or doctrine. The pool meant the Word was stagnant, constrained, and limited; it was not a living, moving Word. The Word of God is a living word, full of motion and purpose.[72] The people in the pool did not know the doctrine was not good; they didn't see that underneath were demons and darkness. The draining of the water was the Spirit of God revealing the falseness of religious doctrines so the truth of the darkness could be seen. God is going to do it.

This dream's message was simple and clear: religion has enveloped this age with a very finite and limited perspective of the Word of God. Little challenges us, requires anything of us, or imparts into us. The reality of our spiritual DNA, the calling to which we are called, or the accountability that we each bear over the life of Jesus Christ, is not something that we are continually made aware of. Rather, we find mental pursuits, moral codes, and the contentment to remain in the confines of (being comfortable in) what we know, even when God would expose it as mere religion.

Here are only a few of the New Testament references that declare that the last days will be full of error; not just potential error, but actual error with consequences and *VICTIMS:*

- Jesus said, "Take heed that no man deceive you. For many shall come in my name, saying, I am Christ; and shall deceive many...And many false prophets shall rise, and shall deceive many. And because iniquity shall abound, the love of many shall wax cold."[73] I believe when the Lord said many would come saying, "I am Christ," He meant that many will come broadcasting a reputation of being anointed.

- "This people draweth nigh unto me with their mouth, and honoureth me with their lips; but their heart is far from me. But in vain they do worship me, teaching for doctrines the commandments of men."[74]

49

This lascivious, light, carefree approach to the gospel is false and exactly the same spirit that was in Nimrod; it declares a contentment to remain in a defined and confined place.[75] So, before we go on and consider in depth where we, "the Church," are now, and how we must go forward, let's go all the way back to Genesis and look at Nimrod and the beginning of Babylon. Why Babylon?

For many years, I have read and reread the scriptures relating to Babylon; many times I have asked the Lord to show me and teach me concerning this subject. During the year of 2018, I began to see certain things about this Babylon. First, it is important; approximately one third of the Bible is given to consideration of the Babylonian experience. Whether in prophecy and forewarning, accounts of God's people in the midst of Babylon, or scriptures that refer to leaving this place of bondage and to the rebuilding of Jerusalem, Scripture devotes an incredible amount of space to this subject.

Why is that so? We know that from Genesis to Revelation, the scriptures are given for the Church's admonition. Upon us is the end of the ages. Why is so much scriptural attention given to this period? As I considered these questions, it began to dawn on me: Babylon was a type of religion. And, religion is dangerous.

CHAPTER 8

BABYLON

BABEL, THE SPIRIT OF BABYLON

The scripture says that you shall know the tree by the fruit that it bears. It is impossible for a corrupt tree to bear good fruit or a good tree to bear corrupt fruit.[76] The firstfruit of Nimrod was Babel in the land of Shinar. Was it a good thing or a bad thing? Let's find out!

The name Nimrod simply means "to be rebellious" or "to revolt."[77] The Bible says, "He began to be a mighty one in the earth."[78] Here the word "began" is the Hebrew word *chalai*, which means "to pollute, desecrate, defile, or profane." Genesis 10:9 states, "He was a mighty hunter before the Lord." The word "mighty" is the Hebrew word *gibbowr*, which means "to magnify oneself, behave proudly, be a tyrant."[79] A hunter is one who takes for food.

These scriptures begin to paint a picture of a man who becomes lifted up in his heart and in his ways and begins a rebellion. It was an open defiance of the good heart of obedience found in Noah. Some commentators feel that the phrase, "a mighty hunter,"[80] describes a pursuit of culture and knowledge; however, the word for "hunter" comes from a verb meaning "to hunt or fish." This scripture would seem to say that Nimrod was not a quiet rebel, but a maker of disciples, a hunter of souls, and a fisher of men.

In Genesis 9:1, the everlasting God said to Noah and his sons, "Be fruitful, and multiply, and replenish the earth." In verse seven, He said, "And you, be ye fruitful, and multiply; bring forth abundantly in the earth, and multiply therein." God gave them a commandment to go and replenish the earth. The earth's population had just been wiped out, and God communicated His expectation that those that were saved would be able to replenish it. This God-given directive had a resulting impact: all of Noah's descendants would be pilgrims in the earth,[81] and that everywhere they went, they would multiply and bring forth.

This commandment also speaks to us in this age of grace. Even as we have been saved by grace, we are saved with the expectation that we go and bring forth fruit and that *our* fruit would remain. For us, "go" is not necessarily a physical going, but it is surely a journey into the Spirit that will last all the days of our lives, into places that we haven't known,[82] where our God becomes all things to us. From this kingdom of heaven, we are able to bring forth eternal fruit to the glory of the Lord Jesus Christ.

Nimrod was a man with true rebellion in his heart, but at that time there wasn't much to rebel against. He had a resistance to the simple life of the nomad, and he began to hate the idea of being a pilgrim for all his days. At first, the contention was internal, but then he began to speak and voice what was in his heart. The more outspoken he became, the more he began to influence others. Soon he had a following; he had sowed the seeds of rebellion, and they began to bring forth a crop.

The scripture says that as they journeyed from the east, they found a plain in the land of Shinar. This is where what Nimrod had sown in his heart came to a head. Genesis 11:2 says, "They dwelt there," with the word "dwelt" coming from the Hebrew *yashab* meaning "to sit down, to marry." The problem with this is the Lord God had commanded them to "journey" to replenish the whole earth. This word "journey" comes from the Hebrew *nasa* meaning literally "to pull up the tent pins." They were not supposed to have a permanent residence.

Instead, they reached a place and time when they would journey no more. It was as if they said, "This is a good place to live; we will not go forth across the whole earth. We will stay here." To travel, to live the life of a pilgrim, means to live the life of struggle, a life of simplicity, usually a life of uncertainty, depending on the provision of God. This was when a people began to manifest the spirit of Nimrod. Now they began to reveal their opposition to the commandment of the Lord God to go forth, multiply, and replenish the earth.

These followers of Nimrod said, "Come let us build a city and a tower, whose top is in the heavens; let us make us a name for ourselves, lest we be scattered abroad over the face of the whole earth. And the Lord came down to see the city and the tower..."[83] Because that people were in unity of action and of one language, He declared that nothing would be kept from them. He purposely confused their language so they couldn't understand one another. Because of that, many began to go forth over the face of the whole earth as the Lord had commanded. This is how the scripture declares it: "Therefore is the name of it called Babel;[84] because the Lord did there confound the language of all the earth: and from thence did the Lord scatter them abroad upon the face of the whole earth."[85]

When they said, "Let us build us a city and a tower," it wasn't just a harmless declaration; surely, this became a place of rebellion against God. "City" here refers to a walled populace, a place protected and defended. This declares that the inhabitants of Babel saw themselves as unique, having a unique perspective, vision, or knowledge.

53

The wall defined that mindset. A tower in Scripture means one's name, the strength of one's name, or being a place of refuge.[86] They not only wanted a name, but they wanted a very significant name. They desired this tower to reach unto the heavens, and all this was done so they would not be scattered across the face of the earth.

This book will purpose to declare several key perspectives plainly; one of those fundamental positions is that Babylon is a type of religion. And, in case you think that I am preoccupied with history, this book takes another key position. The time that we are in right now is an age of religion. We have all been born into, and have continued to live in, this religious age. However, the Holy Spirit of God has begun to open our eyes to the greatness of God's purpose in the Church of the Lord Jesus Christ, particularly this end-time Church. Because of this, I implore us all to not consider Nimrod the outlier or Babel the exception. Nimrod lives in the midst of each one of us, in our carnal nature. To see Babel, we need to look no further than our denomination, sometimes even our own congregation. Let these words, "Get behind Me, Satan! You are an offense to Me, for you are not mindful of the things of God, but the things of men,"[87] be the standard for our perspective regarding these things.

Every place in the heart that resists the call to a simple and consecrated life is no different than the heart that was in Nimrod when he began to rebel. The place where we believe that we know all there is to know about any of a number of different doctrines is a place where we are building the wall of Babel, the wall of religion. Wherever we begin to identify ourselves as this denomination or that movement is no different than laying the bricks in that great tower. It is here that the Lord Himself will allow our speech to be confounded so we cannot understand the congregation down the street, although we are all partakers of one Spirit.

I'm struck by how exactly these descriptions of Babel apply to this present Church age. We see this in how many denominations have sprung up since Azusa Street, each with its unique doctrinal position, its defining wall, its tower. May the Lord help our hearts to be open and consider.

I believe that this ancient Babel is the beginning of religion as we have known it. We can discern this spirit, in this day and age, in a few ways:

- Religion usually has its own plain of Shinar. Most religious doctrine results in an easier way, a lighter burden. Religion has doctrines of ease and prosperity, which actually war against the soul of a man.

- Religion has a distaste for and a fear of the life of the pilgrim; instead, there is a desire for living one's life, with one's identity and fulfilling one's own desires and ambitions.

- The first basic inclination of religion is to build a city—which is defined by having a wall erected around it—and that wall promotes the protecting, defining, the separating, and the excluding of others. Usually the wall is built around a doctrinal position, and that becomes a place of separation in the body of Christ.

- The second inclination is to build a tower—which is to make sure there is a significance to the name of that people. This, in actuality, begins to rival the name of the Lord Jesus. Most would say, "Not me, not us"; however, how many times have we identified ourselves as belonging to this assembly or that doctrine? Instead of taking advantage of precious opportunities to share the gospel of Jesus Christ, many times we first declare our affiliation with a certain doctrine or organization.

- Religion is not vulnerable before God or man but protects its position with pride.

- Religion esteems knowledge more than fellowship in the Spirit. This is so important, because one of the greatest lies of religion is that we relate to our God with our mental approaches. But truthfully, unless we come to know our God in our spirit, we really don't know Him at all. Ours is a place of fellowship in the Spirit,[88] and that is a place of continual revelation.[89]

BABYLON'S MISSING YEARS

Scholars universally recognize that Babel and Babylon are one and the same even though we lose sight of Babel after the book of Genesis. We know historically that Babylon was a prosperous city, disposed to intellectual pursuit and to the establishment of its own moral code. It was a very civilized city with arts and culture,[90] and it is easy to see the spirit of Nimrod there alive and well. One other thing was a trademark of this ancient city—religion.

Religion played a key role in Babylon. At its heart were fourteen different sanctuaries and another twenty-nine scattered throughout the city, in addition to hundreds more street-site chapels and shrines.[91] Babylon took an all-inclusive approach to faith: whatever you believed was okay. Does any of that sound familiar? A very desirable place to live in most people's eyes, Babylon embodied everything good, except the worship of the Almighty God. Scripturally, we pick up Babylon in the reign of Hezekiah, king of Judah.

Hezekiah became king in a time where the nation of Israel had been torn with division. The northern kingdom, called Israel, was known for its wickedness and its evil-hearted kings such as kings Ahab and Jeroboam. They established all manner of abominations equal to all of the heathen nations around them. Although Israel had such a deplorable legacy, in reality, Judah was guilty of the same things.[92] God had begun to speak through the prophet Isaiah about a great destruction He had decreed over Israel and Judah because of their incorrigible ways.

Hezekiah was a good king in a mostly corrupt era of Jewish history. He began to institute sweeping spiritual reform,[93] zealously undoing the evil practices of the kings that went before him. We can really see a lot in looking at this man, but I would like to focus on one of the mistakes that he made.

Hezekiah became sick, and the Lord told him through Isaiah that he was going to die. So, Hezekiah turned to the Lord in prayer, asking for more time, and the Lord granted him an extra fifteen years. While he was recovering from his sickness, the king of Babylon sent Hezekiah a present and well wishes, which King Hezekiah received warmly. This was a mistake because He not only received Babylon's embassage, he showed them all of his riches, all his gold and his silver, all of the spices and the precious ointments, all of his armor, and all of his treasure. He showed them everything in his house and in his domain, with nothing held back.[94]

This was a mistake with grave consequences; he did not see Babylon as a potential enemy. Remember, the world knew Babylon as a city of culture, a place of morals and of knowledge. The Babylonian embassage came to Jerusalem to show King Hezekiah kindness and pleasantries. The king never considered that it was still a heathen nation, and as such, was standing in the position of an adversary.

When Isaiah heard of the visit, he went to King Hezekiah and inquired who these men were, where they came from, and what the king showed them of

Judah. When the king told Isaiah the extent of what was revealed to the Babylonians, Isaiah responded with the word of the Lord. He declared that all the treasures, including everything that had been passed down through the generations, would be taken captive by Babylon. There would be nothing left; even his descendants would become servants of Babylon.[95]

BABYLON'S FIRST DEMAND

This word of the Lord did not come to pass immediately. It was one hundred years after King Hezekiah passed away before the Babylonians came against Jerusalem and besieged it.[96] Nebuchadnezzar, King of Babylon, took all the treasure of the house of the Lord and of the king's house. He also took the golden vessels of the temple and cut them in pieces, and they became plunder for the king of Babylon.

- It is important to carry the concept of Babylon as being a type of religion in our minds because from this point forward we will look at how this Babylon is revealed in our spiritual activities today. Paul, the apostle, referred to the individual believer as being the "temple of God."[97]

- Paul said that we bear this treasure in earthen vessels.[98]

- The vessels of gold and silver reference the godly nature that is formed in those of the Church that overcome their fleshly lineage.[99]

- The Babylonian king took the treasures and the vessels of the temple; but he also took captive the royal people of Judah[100] as well as all that were able to make war,[101] and all those that were craftsmen.[102]

I called this subchapter "Babylon's First Demand" because religion, which Babylon represents, never asks for everything up-front. However, it does first target the gold and the silver that is in the temple. Gold refers to that which is of God or godly; specifically, it refers to where God has developed His nature and character in us. Jesus says to the Church of Laodicea that they should buy of Him gold tried in the fire.[103] Malachi 3:3 says the Lord will sit as a "refiner and purifier of silver," who will purge us as silver and gold. Our faith is called "more precious than gold that perishes."[104] Silver is symbolic of the price of redemption and also of that which can redeem. The more we are changed into the image of Christ, the more the Lord will spend us like money to buy whatever He wants.[105]

The Holy Ghost is working everywhere in the body of Christ to faithfully bring forth His own substance, whether it's His faith, His love, or His faithfulness. However, when we become captive to religious Babylon, these things are rendered useless or nonfunctional. The temple of Christ's "golden vessel" becomes an ornament; it's not used, drawn upon, or valued. Instead, a form of godliness arises; the gold becomes dim.

Notice what else the king of Babylon took captive first. He also took captive the royal people of Judah, all that were able to make war and all those that were craftsmen. In the Church, are we not kings and priests before God? Have we not been given spiritual weaponry? Are we not workers together with God? A craftsman, in the kingdom of heaven, is a spiritual man cloaked in God's wisdom whose every action and word that comes forth is able to change and create. All of these positions are taken captive in religion. They may not be outrightly killed, but constrained, captive, and taught another language.

After this first victory of King Nebuchadnezzar, the wickedness continued in Judah. After about fourteen years, King Nebuchadnezzar returned and laid siege against the city of Jerusalem. This time it was different. This time he didn't want to steal; he wanted to destroy. The siege lasted for two years, and by this time the people of the Lord God could stand no longer.[106] The scripture says that there was no bread for the people; their will broke, and they fled by night from before the Babylonian army.[107] What followed was a revealing of a darker side, *the real spirit of the Babylonians.*

BABYLON'S HEART REVEALED

Do you remember what the scripture said about Nimrod? It says he was mighty before the Lord. His rebellion was not first seen among men, but in the heavenlies, against God Himself. It revealed the hatred that Satan has for God. That hatred is found in the first fruits of Nimrod—Babylon, or religion. Religion is not content to make servants of those that were created to rule with Christ, not content to render the weaponry of the spiritual man ineffective. Neither is it content to cause the labor of faithful men to come to nothing. The hidden agenda for the spirits behind religion is to take from the Father of Lights the very thing that He wants the most, a Bride for His Son.

So, this time when the king of Babylon attacked Judah, he killed the sons of King Zedekiah and put out the eyes of the king of Judah himself. He bound Zedekiah with fetters of brass and carried him away to Babylon. Next, the armies of Nebuchadnezzar burnt the house of the Lord and the king's house and all the houses of Jerusalem; every great man's house was burnt with fire. The armies broke down the walls of Jerusalem with the obvious intent of removing any semblance of Jewish identity as the city of God.

Then the armies beat into pieces and took away to Babylon all the brass of the temple that remained: all the pillars, the utensils, and the brazen sea. It was so much brass that the scripture declares it was brass without number.[108] A word here: sometimes we are so concerned with the silver and the gold that we give no thought to that which is made of brass. Brass is similar to gold but just not as precious. It can be beaten, formed, take on the image of something, and be buffed to a dazzling brilliance; but, it can also tarnish. According to the plan of God, David provided brass without weight for the temple.

I believe the Holy Spirit showed me that brass in the temple represents the works of righteousness that we do in our earthly bodies. These are not works of self-righteousness, but of our obedience to the Spirit of God while in our earthly tabernacle. They are valued by God and accepted by mercy and grace. When Babylon took away all the brass of the temple, it declared a very evil effect of religion: Religious people become bound in a motionless existence that does not require, or make room for, works of righteousness. We become an emaciated people where our faith and love are weakened through lack of use.

Lastly, the captain of the Babylonians took seventy-two Israelites/Jews and slew them in Syria. What a sad judgement that the holy people of God had come to such a complete and utter end. Everything that marked them as the people of God was taken away, destroyed, or burnt with fire. It's no wonder that the prophet Jeremiah, who saw all this happen, is often called the "Weeping Prophet."

CHAPTER 9

WHERE IS THE GOLD AND THE SILVER?

I write this next chapter thinking about the brethren that I know and have known whose lights are fading. My heart hurts for the elderly brethren who have been so faithful in the place where they were called so long ago and now are preparing to move on into eternity. Some of these brethren are not rejoicing in the race they have run or in the fruit they have brought forth. More than a few of these had received words of purpose, visions of labors, and ministries many years ago by the Holy Spirit; yet after all of these years, they have not walked in these callings. If they were lazy spiritually, I could see it. If Christ had not been not formed in them, it would be easy to understand. One could perhaps explain this as being the wisdom of our God who brings forth every generation as it pleases Him, except for one thing. Sadness is in the hearts and eyes of many of these elderly brothers and sisters in Christ. Somehow what has taken place in their lifetime has not revealed what the Holy Ghost had sown into their hearts.

Is it possible that these were not encouraged to manifest and flow in the gifts that God had given them? Has nobody ever inquired of these concerning their hope? It may or may not be too late to manifest many of these callings, but I am positive of this: there is a place in the heavenlies that we all can inhabit and bring forth fruit no matter our age. May Babylon lose its hold over the spiritual substance of these aged brethren, and may we, the body of Christ, begin to desire after the wisdom and understanding of our fathers.[109]

Not far behind these are those who, like me, are firmly embracing middle age. Many of us have been walking with the Lord for many years, and I cannot tell you of the struggles I have encountered personally, and how many times hope has almost left me. Not a hope of salvation, but rather a hope that comes from an inherent desire to bless and profit the kingdom of God. If a person has the substance of Christ worked in him, that person is as an ox, ready to labor. He is as an eagle that soars above the activities of this realm, and he is as a lion that is hungry to destroy the works of the devil.

Many fall into these earthly and spiritual age brackets yet are constrained. I have also seen in this age men that are ready, faithful in their fellowship with God, and yet they battle hopelessness. It's in their eyes, in their walk, and in their spirit. May the Holy Spirit set these free, and may they go forth in strength and in purpose, to build again the temple of the Lord and see the wall of Jerusalem once again established. Hallelujah!

Next, I look at those who are in their thirties and forties and firmly entrapped by the cares of this world and the deceitfulness of riches. These labor without ceasing to uphold a standard of living, send their kids to college, and to be able to take certain times of leisure. Yet all the while, a calling and a purpose in them gives them no true peace. This drawing of the Holy Spirit isn't defined, and sometimes it isn't clear, but it is surely there. These feel the vanity of their lives but don't see a path forward.

Remember the trademark prosperity of ancient Babylon, and remember also their pursuit of knowledge. Now consider the gold and the silver vessels that were separated in Babylon from their ordained functions. Oh, that this generation would see through the lies of religion and understand the purpose of God for their lives. I have watched some start their journey of faith, with God working mightily to change and strengthen them. But now, they seem to have faltered, and their fire has apparently been reduced to only embers.

We can't lose a generation! I speak bluntly to these young men of Christ;[110] we cannot do this without you. The Church of the living God must rise up with renewed strength and build. We need the strength and the zeal of this generation that is coming of age. "Wherefore lift up the hands which hang down, and the feeble knees; and make straight paths for your feet, lest that which is lame be turned out of the way; but let it rather be healed."[111]

My heart is drawn heavily toward those in their teens and twenties. Many times it feels to me like this is the group that needs God's touch the most. Now is the time in their lives where strong attractions rise up that can result in lives full of frustration and misdirection. This is the time where the input and the doctrines of the world most heavily influence these young souls. Remember what Babylon did to the young, elite men of Judea? They were taught the learning and tongue of the Chaldeans, a language of prosperity and knowledge. Does that ring a bell? Who will reaffirm the tongue of holiness and school these in the presence of God?

Another thing that affects these young people, possibly more than any other, is the separation that comes with religion. Remember the wall of Babylon, how it isolates and segregates? How many young people have looked around their congregation, their denomination, and have seen no one they could walk with? Many times little opportunity exists for friendship, exhortations, or even marriage, and the result is that many fall away. A block away, a town away, other congregations have young people with the exact same issues. Separation makes us all vulnerable, but none more so than these young adults.

Then, there are the children—the future of the Church. These are the most vulnerable and also those who possibly have the most potential. Their spirits are simple and cry out to know God, but so often they lack the impact of the holy presence of God. Their whole lives lie ahead of them, but few have a role model that will anchor and train them in the way they should go. So precious and so beautiful are those that do have a spiritual presence in their lives and have already learned to pray and worship.

I know one more group that religion has affected: the broken, the cast-offs, and the disillusioned. There have been so many Church splits, so much contention, so many adulteries, and so much ego in the ministry positions of today's churches. All of these things have wounded, broken, and blinded souls, almost without number. These are sons with spiritual substance, filled with the Spirit of the Living God and groomed by His Spirit; yet now, they are broken, discarded, and forgotten. They no longer see their gold and silver in the temple of the Lord Jesus Christ; their heavenly purpose is forgotten by all but our heavenly Father.[112]

I heard a preacher of a flourishing church tell of how he had sought counsel after a group of people left his congregation. The counseling pastor, who is highly regarded in the country, told him this concerning those who left: "Sometimes God just has to flush the toilet."

I know none of the details of this particular happening, but I know that I physically recoiled when I heard that, repulsed in my spirit. I heard another preacher declare recently, "As long as you are breathing, there is hope." These broken and disillusioned people are possibly weak in faith but are absolutely not refuse. They are neither forgotten nor discarded by our heavenly Father.

So, from old to young, across the board, the Holy Spirit has given gifts and has purposed to work His own nature and character into the earthen vessels of the redeemed. His Church is purposed to be extravagantly wealthy in spiritual things, revealing Almighty God Himself. When you look around, how much gold and how much silver do you see? How much hopelessness and weakness in the spirits of the redeemed?[113] Babylon has made her first request, but her real spirit is yet to be seen![114]

There may be a temptation to view the present state of the Church with something less than alarm, not discerning the slow and steady advance of darkness in the Church. This would be a very grave mistake because, although we are clearly now in a state of religion that is foretold in Babylon's first invasion of Judah, a revelation remains of the true spirit of Babylon: the antichrist incarnate![115]

A spirit that is dark, sinister, and hates our God is at work in religion, empowering it. This Satanic spirit wants nothing less than to utterly destroy the temple of God, break down the wall of the Church (that precious hope that identifies us as Christ's), and kill all of the priesthood (persecution). This spirit of antichrist desires to take all the brass (all of the right responses to the Spirit of God that the sons of God do while in our earthly tabernacles) and break it in pieces and take it as spoil. All the mighty men of this hour will be targeted. *It is impossible to overestimate the evil of the spirit that is behind the present state of the Church.*

CHAPTER 10

APOSTASY

I want to talk about the current state of the Church as the Holy Spirit has revealed it to me. The king of Babylon has not stopped with creating a little frustration; neither is he content with causing a little hopelessness in the people of God. He is currently conducting subtle and not so subtle campaigns to change the Church. No longer are we a people having a well-defined faith in a most holy God. Rather, we have become a people having a thousand variations of a belief that makes God just like us, leaving no need for us to change, be transformed, or have eternal accountability.

This attack has not just begun; it has been in motion since the days of the apostles. Now, however, things are moving more quickly, directly, with less disguise, forcing the body of Christ to give ground and to accept as normal things contrary to scripture. I would like to share here another dream the Lord gave me about two years ago:

> I was in a house with some other people; however, they weren't the focus of the dream. As we went about our daily living, someone found a snake in the house. It was coiled up, and I recognized it as a poisonous variety. I threw a piece of cloth over it and took it outside. I was unafraid but very careful because I knew it was deadly.

Outside was a small lawn and beyond were woods. A small body of crystal-clear water, which I had to walk by to let the snake go, was on the edge of the woods. Walking by the pond, which was so crystal clear I could see all the rocks on its bottom, I looked into the water and saw a huge serpent's head nested among the rocks. It looked like a very large anaconda's head. I could see it watching me. When it realized that I had seen it, it began to move toward me. I backed away, not afraid but very watchful. As it came out of the water, it stood up on its back legs, like a very large, lizard-like creature, about eight-to-ten feet tall.

I returned to the house after releasing the snake, and upon moving from room to room, I began to find more snakes, all of them venomous. There were a number of varieties; all were coiled but not attacking.

There was also a cute lion cub, maybe about fifty pounds, and I commenced to move it outside. It was a handful. I finally got it out the door and then tried to shut the door behind him. The second the cub was on the other side of the door, it turned into a very strong, full-grown lion. It fought to get back in. I struggled to close the door, but something wasn't right. As I was struggling, I turned my head and saw that all the hinge screws on the door were removed except one. It flashed through my mind that the door had been sabotaged, and that's why the house was full of serpents.

There was a brief moment before the door closed that my head was outside, and I looked to the left. I could see that the house was sitting on a small hill. Down below, what looked like a patch of lawn, like a ballfield, was lit up with lights because it was nighttime. From that patch of lawn, a steady stream of people came walking up the hill toward me. It seemed for a second that they meant harm because their demeanor was so sober; however, they walked on by, with scarcely a look, and continued on into the darkness.

The Interpretation, as Much as I Have of it:

The house is the Church. The cloth that I threw over the serpent is the righteousness of Christ. The body of water, next to the woods, is a doctrine that seems to be truth (the water of the pool was crystal clear and looked very clean). But in its depths, hidden among the rocks, lies the greatest of all serpents, Satan. As soon as I became aware of it, it became combative. Changing its shape, it stood up on its back legs aggressively and came toward me. I believe this refers to a time of persecution coming against the true Church.

The snakes represent both people and doctrines that are dangerous and poisonous. They were positioned to strike but at present undiscovered. The lion cub is a practice that Satan has established in the Church that seems quite acceptable, tolerable, even enjoyable. However, when thrust outside the Church, it revealed itself as a full-grown, very strong lion that fought to regain its position in the Church.

The door, with the hinge screws missing, alludes to certain elements of the doctrine of the crucified Christ that have been removed over time. I believe one of these missing screws is the element of holiness. If we remove holiness from the gospel,[116] the way gets broader and the gospel of Christ is easier to accept. There is less of a requirement to overcome individual sin, and we lose the need to be in the presence of God. Removing these

71

screws, which are critical to the effectiveness of the door, allows the door to appear to be hanging as normal. However, it no longer works the way it was intended as a barrier; in contrast, it now allows snakes and lions to enter and lie in wait.

Lastly, the people that I saw were not joyful (in that brief second, they seemed like a team that had played a hard game and lost), and they walked as a steady stream out of the light of this world into the darkness of eternity. The Church was right in their path, but they barely looked and probably had not even noticed it.

This dream revealed several incredible things:

- There are serpents in the house.[117]

- We have provided a place given to Satan (the cute lion cub) in the midst of our worship.[118]

- The door, which I believe is the doctrine of the crucified Christ, has been sabotaged. It appeared to be hanging as usual, but when I tried to open it, it no longer functioned the way the Father intended.[119]

- Nothing about the Church arrested the sinners as they walked by on the way into the darkness of eternity.[120]

- A time of persecution will begin for the Church when we see where Satan's seat is. I believe that Satan's seat is a place of strong influence where he can influence the spiritual well-being of each generation of believers. Somehow, he is presently still undiscovered in the midst of mainstream doctrine. I believe we all see some snakes, but a great presence is hidden.

It is not my intent for this book to be a discourse about doctrine and doctrinal differences, for that is one of the greatest reasons for this mess that the Church is in. Many of the schisms in the Church today come from issues that should not divide brother from brother. Surely the love of God is able to make us honor and walk with our brethren no matter our differences.

Our doctrinal differences come out of a place of revelation that is not complete in itself and should not be used as a sword to kill our brethren that are filled with the same Holy Ghost as we. For many years, I have been listening and have heard that even within one doctrinal camp, no one speaks exactly the same thing. That in itself is not alarming because every one of us occupies a different room in the house of God. We only have pieces of the great revelation of the glory of God.[121] Now is not the time to become preoccupied with our doctrinal differences, but rather to become occupied with the pursuit of the presence of our Lord and God!

All godly doctrine is to help the sons of God, the brethren of the Lord Jesus Christ, to grow in grace and truth. This new covenant is all about fellowship with our God in the Spirit; to fellowship with our God, we must become truth.

But some things have become mainstream in America's Church that are absolutely not scriptural. The effects of these doctrinal positions are potentially influencing the eternal destiny of millions of souls. Any doctrine that is not conducive to us becoming *disciples* of the Lord Jesus is not a godly doctrine and should be examined and put out of the household of faith. However, how can we examine a doctrine without division?

Recently, I had the privilege to attend a ministry seminar hosted by Bishop Joseph Matera. He conducted it in such a manner that I left the seminar very much increased in hope. There was a position of honor one toward another when those present discussed each verse of Scripture. What an atmosphere for apologetics! That alone offered me a hope of consensus on critical doctrinal issues and an alternative to the separation seen in today's Church.

So, how do we answer this onslaught of darkness, this spiritual warfare being warred against us? How do we not only push back the darkness but see a complete transformation come upon the Church? How do we see ourselves and those we love put on the glory of God and become the manifest Bride of Christ, fulfilling the desire of our heavenly Father? I believe answers lie in the books of Ezra and Nehemiah.

CHAPTER 11

REBUILD THE WALLS
REBUILD THE TEMPLE
– THE VISION OF NEHEMIAH

My wife and I came to a place where we were led to leave the congregation we had attended for thirty-five years. We left with no idea where to go and more than a little scared at the uncertainty of what lay before us. What followed was a four-month journey, from congregation to congregation, our only directive being "to see what the Lord had invested in His people." As we went, the Holy Spirit began to deal with me out of the book of Nehemiah. Nehemiah was a Jew who was a servant to the king of Persia during the time of the Babylonian captivity. He heard about the state of the temple in Jerusalem and how the city was defenseless with its walls torn down. Nehemiah was also informed concerning the remnant of Jews that were yet in Jerusalem, and he became overcome by the reproach of it.

In summary, Nehemiah got permission from the king of Persia to go to Jerusalem and rebuild its wall.[122] When he got there, his first order of business was not to hold a meeting and discuss things. Rather, he got up in the middle of the night while everyone slept and travelled about what was left of the city wall, surveying the extent of the damage. He took measure of such, and when he met with the elders the next day, he began to speak of the vision that God had given him. He called on the elders to begin to work together to rebuild the walls of the holy city.

I have heard my pastor, Raffoul Najem, say that Nehemiah represents the Holy Spirit. If that is so, then He has surely been checking out every facet of the Church while men slept. He knows exactly what is broken, what has been stolen, and who has learned the language of the Babylonians. He not only knows this, but He also has a plan[123] and has begun to call the elders of the Church to prepare to rebuild the temple and the walls of the new Jerusalem. By "rebuilding the temple," I mean the Holy Spirit has begun calling His people to strong prayer. In addition, He is causing them to desire places of true worship in the Spirit. The Holy Spirit is also awakening His people to see the walls of the New Jerusalem rebuilt. Remember, this speaks to sanctification and being a people with a unique identity. Also, the wall declares that the people are a people protected.

As my wife and I traveled, we saw how in each congregation there were the good, the bad, and the ugly; no assembly had been perfected. We saw no perfect praise, no perfect word, no perfect love; in every congregation, we saw a generation of God's people that needed to go on. The Church could not stay where it was, as our God was looking for more. I felt the vision of Nehemiah being birthed in the depths of my soul.

As I poured over the book of Nehemiah, reading it a number of times, I became very aware of certain key points:

- It was Jerusalem that was destroyed, its wall broken down and burnt with fire. I know that Jerusalem speaks to the Church of this age of grace.[124] I know the wall of Jerusalem refers to that spiritual separation of today's believer and unbeliever, all those who are in grace from all those who are without. The wall thereby creates the uniqueness of the people which inhabit the Church—the spiritual Jerusalem. Even as Jerusalem's broken wall provided no safety and no definition of the Jewish identity, so the Church's uniqueness has faded. The lines between it and the world have blurred, and the Church is a hair's breadth away from becoming part of the confusion of this age.

- The Israelites' unity of labor in the face of opposition reminds me of the unity of labor that I had experienced in the rebuilding of my friend's mobile home. I know that I saw great humility and great love for the brethren in that project, and I'm positive that is a key ingredient in building again the broken walls of this spiritual Jerusalem.[125]

- Nehemiah was stirred, not only to pray, but also to rise up and work. There is a time to talk, and there is a time for the Church to put its money where its mouth is. For years I have professed and lived some degree of a spiritual reality. What that degree is, I can't judge. This, however, I can judge: now is the time for Paul Kimball to leave those things which are behind and reach for those things which are ahead and to press toward the mark of the high calling of God that is in Christ Jesus.[126] I, and I believe also the whole Church, must sell out and follow the Holy Spirit into abandonment.

- All those that labored with Nehemiah were glad for the prosperity of Jerusalem. They rejoiced greatly in spite of their weariness and the continual threatening of the enemy. What was the cause of this joy? They believed they were pursuing, stone by stone, the welfare of the people of God and the city of God. Why should we today be content to have

77

honor and security ourselves and the house of the Lord our God lie in waste?[127]

• There was a place of separation from the world, a renewal of tithing, and a casting out of every unclean element that was found during the labor of Nehemiah and the restoring of Jerusalem. Nehemiah, in restoring the Temple, found a large room that was previously used for storing the tithes, meat offerings, and the holy vessels. The chief priest, however, had given it as a permanent residence to Tobiah, a hater of God. When Nehemiah found out, he was grieved. He cast Tobiah out and all of his belongings with him. Nehemiah's jealous heart for God needs to be manifested in today's Church.

Here are several examples of how these points apply to this age of grace:

The Church has so much in common with the world that it's very difficult to know the difference. We dress the same, eat and drink the same, and have the same dependence on entertainment, sports, and music. This is not music that is worship to God, but that which satisfies *our* individual souls.

We have fulfilling careers that drain our energy. We desire money and the comforts it provides for us and find security in our 401Ks that allow us to enjoy leisure in retirement.

Our desire in finding a husband or wife is more often based on beauty and what he or she has to offer financially than about their spiritual vision, the purpose of their lives, and how mature they are in the Spirit.

One of the greatest needs we have in committing to the restoring of the Church is to become faithful with our money. Many sermons have declared that if God has our heart, then He has our money. If we aren't tithing and involved in sacrificial giving to the work of God, it certainly shows that our hearts are more committed to our own interests than the interests of God and His kingdom.

There are many things in today's Church that do not show honor toward the name of Jesus or to the life of God. I know we can speak to a number of things here, but one thing that makes me groan personally is the place the clock has in our worship. Does everyone know that this is not how it is supposed to be? How can we worship God for a set time only?

The temple of Solomon was entirely destroyed, the gold and silver vessels were stolen, and the brass was broken in pieces and taken away. The furnishings of the temple were taken or hidden, and the whole structure was burnt with fire. Finally, even the stones of the temple were torn down and strewn in the streets of the city. What is the entirety of what Ezra and Nehemiah's vision to rebuild the temple and the wall mean for us who live in this time? How can we rebuild if we don't see what is broken or stolen? We can't unless the Spirit of God shows us, and that won't happen without intercession.

Even after we begin to understand the great work that lies ahead, we can do nothing without prayer. Not one thing can be done in our own strength. If the Lord doesn't build the house, its builders labor in vain.

CHAPTER 12

THE CALL TO INTERCESSION

Three years ago, while my wife and I spent a short period visiting different congregations, we felt our mission was to see what God had invested in His people. During this time, the Holy Spirit began to show me many things about the Church and ancient Babylon, and I began to understand the immensity of the spiritual crisis that God's people are in. This was not a matter for individuals; this would require a holy people on their knees, crying out for the mercy and grace of God to be poured forth. Very literally, if our God doesn't do this work, this work won't be done!

I have told this story a number of times, but it's the only way I know to describe the position of how the whole body of Christ can move out of bondage and into the truth and reality of our salvation. We had been at our new place of worship for about five months, and my wife and I began to get discouraged. There was such a need of prayer that it seemed hopeless. One day, as I lifted this up to the Lord in prayer, the Holy Spirit spoke this to me. "Paul, there is not one door in heaven that is closed to you. Change it! Stop hanging out in unbelief and get it done!" It's been two years since that time, and the congregation is slowly being changed into a praying church.

Vessels of prayer are beginning to come together, and it's holy. You can feel the cry in their spirits; things are building in strength and might. It's change!

The same word goes forth to all the children of God. If we, God's children, are drawing a breath in this age, we are breathing with one purpose and one call: to throw off the chains of religion and put on the chains of love toward our God. His will must be done! From this position, let's undertake the work ahead. It's time to stop complaining and realize that God is looking for partners in this last labor. All things are possible, if we only believe!

HOLINESS

One of the most important things that we need to look at when it comes to intercession is holiness. This is not just for us to see a great and glorious change break forth in the Church without us being changed individually. God will hear our prayer of faith wherever we are, but our first prayer must be for our heavenly Father to draw us to Himself and grant us a place of repentance.[128] Why repentance? The scripture says that the way of every man is right in his own eyes, but the Lord tries the spirit.[129] It also says that you will know the tree by the fruit.[130] There is, quite probably, more grace given to us as individuals than what we are actually walking in. The letters to the churches in Asia, written by the Apostle John, exemplify this thought. Every church had something that was unacceptable to the holiness of the Lord Jesus Christ; every church was admonished.[131] If this is true, then we all become needy, and we are all called to change. Also, by the very definition of grace, we have the power within us to change.

I believe what God is looking for is a people that desire Him so much that they are willing to leave this world and all it offers behind in order to serve Him anyway He wishes. This is not just emotional desire that He's looking for, but to see His own holiness in us.[132]

I had a dream a long time ago concerning the process of increasing in holiness:

> I stood on a hill and looked out over a plain, and out of the plain a massive butte rose up. Its height was towering above the hill that I stood on, and the side that faced me appeared to be very sheer with no apparent way a person could climb it. I looked to the right, and I could see people making their way up this cliff, but they weren't even using their hands. There appeared to be steps from bottom to top, and these people were ascending that sheer face, one step at a time, using only their feet. It was a sight that defied logic, and when I inquired of the Lord, I felt like He said, "This rock is My holiness, and the steps are one obedient response after another."

This is what the scripture means when it says for us to yield our members as servants of righteousness unto holiness.[133] The Holy Ghost will transform us into the very image of God if we obey Him. So, for this great labor of prayer that we're looking at, we want to be a golden bowl of incense—a holy vessel of prayer, clothed in His own nature and character. Out of that place, let the waters flow!

UNITY

Another thing that must be part of this great work of intercession is unity. The movement of intercession can begin small. It can start with one believer, or it can start with a small group. However, one thing is sure; it will be with a people in agreement approaching our God as a united people. This in itself is rare, and anytime we've seen this throughout history, we've also seen revival. I feel thankful for everyone who prays and for every prayer warrior, but by the power of God, we need to come now as a people.

Concerning my friend's mobile home, something spectacular, something very prophetic was taking place. I saw individuals, that were quite possibly more qualified than I was, take a lower position because God had put it in my heart to be a blessing to this man. One by one these people humbled themselves and fit in wherever they were needed; it really was incredible! Think of this: for four months, we worked in every kind of weather, doing every kind of work. I never once heard a cross word, never saw any eyebrows raised to question decisions, and never heard a complaint from anyone, other than the battles of faith that took place within myself.

This last move of the Spirit is not going to be about us as individuals, and it's not going to be about me or mine. Most definitely, it will be about humility, honor, and brotherly love. That's what it will take to bring forth unity, and it will take unity to bring forth this last push of the Spirit[134] to bring forth the Bride of Christ. Blessed be the name of our heavenly Father!

I gave the following prophecy that relates to this work of intercession on Sunday morning, May 5th, 2020, during a time of corporate prayer:

> I have raised up men that are able to take their place, able to take their place (as laborers in this work of rebuilding). I've already done this, because this work doesn't start with you, My sons; it starts with Me. Whosoever will, draw near to Me with your whole heart and see what I will do. Unto the holy am I going to do this; not unto the unholy, but unto the holy. As I begin to move in the midst of the holy, unholy shall rise up and begin to persecute. Do not fear, and do not stand in a place of drawing back; but with all of your heart and all of your soul, finish this work, My sons, finish it, finish it, finish it!

I speak it, I speak it, I speak it, I speak it. My blood is in you, my Son's blood is in you. I have given you everything that you need; stand as men, stand as strong men and understand that for this hour have you been ordained. For this hour have you come! I declare life unto you, I declare blessing unto you, that you might do this work and stand before Me as holy vessels. Stand as all that I am and call upon my name to do this work. You will give me license to do something that has never been done; this is your mission. My blood is in you. My blood is in you; My holy blood. I declare life, I declare life![135]

CHAPTER 13

THE BRIDE

What can be said about the Bride of Christ? Does she represent hope to an era of God's people like Queen Esther did to the Israelites? Is our inclusion in the Bride based on the confession of our mouths or the confession of our lives? Is all that we call the "Church" part of that heavenly Bride? Here are several things that I know for sure concerning the Bride of Christ:

She is in love with her husband

The Song of Solomon sets forth an allegory about how the Church loves her husband. She loves His presence, His smell, His ways, and His Word. She is passionate in her love, and when she is out of His presence, she runs and searches for Him. Nothing can prevent her; nothing can keep her from Him.

The Lamb's wife will search Him out in the life of each soul; every time she sees His nature or His character in someone, the doors of her heart are opened instantly, and she loves passionately. Faithfully, she serves her brethren because they have the similitude of her husband-to-be.

She's without spot or blemish

Her heart is lowly; she is aware that she is redeemed from darkness. Always her heart bows before the whisper of the Spirit of God, and trembling is in her way. He speaks, and she listens and obeys. Obedience by obedience, she changes; her ways change, her nature changes. Her garment is washed by the Word of God; correction is her portion. She continues pressing toward her holy, spotless presentation.[136]

She's faithful to her husband

She stands when all those around her would fall. Family, friends—all may fall. But her eyes are fixed on the will of God, and she is unmovable. Sickness comes on her and will not depart, but she will not speak accusation against her God. She endures difficulties, defeats, and oppositions, but she trusts in her God. Confusion and darkness, uncertainties and exaltations; everything purposes to move her, but she refuses. Nothing matters more than her place of fellowship; she will not let go.[137] In her patience, she possesses her soul.

She is clothed with fine linen

The Lamb's wife has learned obedience by the things she has suffered. She doesn't care for the comforts of her own life. Her eye is quick to see others' needs. Everything she has, she will give, if by any chance those she helps will put on strength. She doesn't desire earthly wealth, but she understands the value of what lives in her. All things are possible; she will pray and not let her countenance fall. Until her last breath, she works gathering souls and raising children of the kingdom. Her children rise up and call her blessed. She is clothed with fruitfulness. Her garment is white and clean, for the fine linen is the righteousness of the saints.[138]

All of this takes me back to where it began—rebuilding a mobile home with brethren from five different congregations. Was this the Lamb's Bride? The glorious Bride is not defined by denomination, affiliation, or doctrine.

It is defined by the love of the brethren, faithfulness, and a right response to the Spirit of God. Step by step, we come forth out of every kindred and every nation. The Lord Jesus Christ will have His Bride, and our heavenly Father will rest!

Final Thoughts

To me, this seems so clear: we are a people with such an incredibly high calling. We are called to leave all that we've known and journey into all that God is. Called to die to all that we have known and live unto all that God has known. Called unto purity where everything of darkness, everything of this world passes away, leaving only the clean and holy. Called to manifest the dominion of the Lord Jesus Christ Himself while we are yet in this earth. Called to bring forth fruit and have that fruit remain forever and ever. Hallelujah!

Such is our calling, but we are waking to find that such is not our present state. How then do we fulfill our heavenly calling? How do we awake completely from our slumber? How can we see our hearts change and the zeal of the Lord break forth in the Church? How can we possibly be freed from all that hinders and all that has influenced us in error? In the midst of affluence, how do we shoulder the cross? To me, the answer lies in the parable of the widow and the unjust judge.[139] Like the widow, who persistently demanded justice from the judge, if we will consistently pray and ask for God's help in every area of our need, He is faithful to answer us. Bit by bit, we will be changed.

Recently the Holy Ghost said to me, "Your ministry is a ministry of exhortation." I believe that's what this book is all about. Exhorting God's people to do a thing, rallying the Bride of Christ to get ready. It's the sound of the shofar to God's people. It's not meant to be a teaching, and it's not necessarily an exposé. The book needs to convey exhortation, or its mission is not finished.

Even though we are so blessed of God in this salvation that we enjoy, we really can't do anything in our own strength. We can't assume positions of an intercessor or a prayer warrior. We don't love God enough, and we don't love our brethren enough; everything about us is limited. Everything has to be increased. We have to begin to cry out for God to give us His heart—a true desire for souls and for His will. Every step of the way, intercession will be like that. We're never going to say that since we're intercessors, we'll do this, or we'll do that. Intercession is a place of desperation; a place of extreme need and a place of knowing that without Him we can't do anything at all. Our first and abiding position is to cry out, "God, help me! God, help us love! Help us desire to do this work; help me, help us."

My wife Rochelle asked, "Do you think these things are opened to us gradually?"

I answered, "Yes, I do. A lot of these times where we cry out for God's help are times where God will answer us according to His purpose that He sees fermenting in us. He proves us in these places, and it can be a gradual, progressive thing. He is not frantic or desperate, and He doesn't just pour out His treasures if we are not positioned to steward them. Because we are naturally proud, consider ourselves highly, and believe our ways are right in our own eyes, so it feels like we should be able to just do this work of intercession. But I am positive our first position of intercession has to be one of humility and truth. Our spirit and our life must say, 'God, in my own strength, I cannot do what must be done! I absolutely need you.'"

I was recently considering Elijah after he slayed the prophets of Baal. Scripture says that after he prayed, he got up, girded himself, and ran before the chariots of Ahab.[140] The Spirit of the Lord caught him up, and he ran before the horses. That's what needs to happen to us. The Spirit of the Lord needs to catch us up and begin to move us.

He says that He works within us "to will and to do of His good pleasure."[141] I believe if someone hears this word and recognizes it as a word from the Spirit, and the Spirit kindles desire in him to respond rightly to it, then it's the Spirit of God who has moved in him. It's so important that we recognize our need for Jesus and for grace to abound over us so that we begin to call out for God to avenge us. Avenge us of our hardness of heart, avenge us of our unbelief, avenge us of all the things that are at work in our members, that work in the midst of the body of Christ. Avenge us of these things, deliver us from these things, these oppressors, these accusers; deliver us from these things.

Scripture says that God will do that thing speedily.[142] Nevertheless, will He find faith when He returns? To me, that passage says it all. We are called to stand in all of these places of change that are before us. We must begin to exercise this childlike faith and cry out to our heavenly Father, "Daddy, help me!" Exercise that. It's not that we stand as princes and kings and within our power try to do all things. It's really that we say, "Father, I need Your help; I'm not seeing this in me." It feels like this message of humility and brokenness of spirit cannot be overemphasized in this book. It's not about what we can do. We can only be vessels; the power to change us and the Church is the Lord's. Hallelujah!

Keys – Symbols

- Gold refers to deity, to God.
  Exodus 37:17-22; Isaiah 13:12; Lamentations 4:2

- Silver refers to price of redemption or the redeemed.
  Exodus 21:32; Zechariah 11:12-13

- Brass refers to the works or ways of righteousness that God's people do as they follow the Holy Spirit.
  Revelation 1:15, 2:18

- Jerusalem refers to the Church and to the Bride of Christ.
  Revelation 3:12, 21:2,10

- Vessels refer to man as carrying, or not carrying, the eternal gifts of God.
  1 Thessalonians 4:4; 2 Timothy 2:20-21

- The temple refers to the individual believer as well as the corporate body in Christ.
  1 Corinthians 3:16, 6:19; Revelation 21:22; 1 Peter 2:5

- Food or bread refers to the Word made flesh.
  John 6:33,35; 1 Corinthians 5:8

- Royalty refers to the heritage of Christ.
  1 Timothy 6:15; 1 Peter 2:9

- The rich refers to those with great gifting or callings.
  Ephesians 1:18; James 2:5

- Poor refers to those that have little substance.
  Revelation 3:17

- Strong men refer to the mature in spirit.
  1 Corinthians 16:13; Romans 15:1; 1 John 2:14

- Craftsmen refer to the laborers, those that have grace to do.
  1 Corinthians 3:10; Romans 9:21

- The walls of Jerusalem refer to protection, separation, and identity.
  Proverbs 18:11; Isaiah 5:5, 60:18

- Stones refer to the redeemed of the Lord.
  1 Peter 2:5

- Fire can mean judgement or trial.
  1 Peter 1:7, 4:12

- High places refer to the vain imaginations of men worshiping in the high places; it means to give value and attention to the same things that the lost do.
  2 Corinthians 2:5

- Passing through the fire is the sacrificing of the first born to strange gods.
  Ezekiel 20:26

- Adultery
  Ezekiel 16, Matthew 5:28

ENDNOTES

1. Galatians 3:28
2. Genesis 1:26
3. Matthew 3:17; Hebrews 1:2
4. Romans 8:32
5. Psalms 139:1-16; Ephesians 1:22
6. Hebrews 12:23
7. Matthew 5:8; 1 John 3:3
8. Ephesians 4:13-16
9. Ephesians 5:27; Song of Solomon 4:7; 2 Corinthians 11:2
10. Genesis 5:2
11. 1 Peter 3:4
12. 2 Corinthians 3:17-18
13. Luke 13:24
14. Exodus 21:5-6
15. Luke 9:23
16. John 1:14
17. Hebrews 2:14-15
18. Psalms 74:2; Titus 2:14
19. Isaiah 35:6-7; Isaiah 49:8-10
20. John 2:21; 1 Corinthians 3:16
21. Ephesians 2:21
22. Hebrews 9:7-9,24; Hebrews 10:19-20
23. *http://www.ldolphin.org/TMTRS.html*
24. Hebrews 9:3; John 4:23-24
25. 1 Corinthians 13:7
26. Romans 8:28-30; Hebrews 10:11-12; Titus 3:5
27. Genesis 6:6
28. Genesis 6:8
29. Genesis 13:14-15
30. Genesis 15:13; Acts 7:6

[31] Matthew 4:16-17,23

[32] Isaiah 63:1-4

[33] John 1:14

[34] Hebrews 1:2-3

[35] *https://www.travelujah.com/stories/who-were-galileans-days-jesus*

[36] John 8:29

[37] Matthew 16:23 (NKJV)

[38] Matthew 17:21 (NKJV)

[39] Luke 12:1 (NKJV)

[40] Mark 12:17 (NKJV)

[41] John 15:13 (NKJV)

[42] Luke 24:49 (NKJV)

[43] Acts 2:1

[44] Acts 1:8, Luke 24:49

[45] Acts 2:42-46

[46] Acts 2:43; Acts 5:11

[47] Acts 17:6

[48] Act 15:1,7

[49] 2 Timothy 2:18

[50] 1 Corinthians 1:11-12; Galatians 1:6-8

[51] Romans 1:18-32; 1 Corinthians 3:3, 5:1; James 4:1-4

[52] Joshua 24:31 (NKJV)

[53] Judges 2:10

[54] Acts 6:4

[55] Isaiah 6:5; Hebrews 12:21; Daniel 10:8-11

[56] John 6:63; 2 Corinthians 3:6

[57] 1 Samuel 8:19

[58] Exodus 20:21

[59] 1 Samuel 8:6

[60] 1 Samuel 8:7

[61] Isaiah 62:4-5

[62] Mathew 23:37

63 Deuteronomy 27:7; Psalms 105:43

64 1 Corinthians 10:6,11

65 1 John 2:27; John 10:4-5,27

66 Acts 6:4

67 1 Kings 19:18; Luke 2:36; Luke 2:25-27

68 Acts 2:1-13 (NKJV)

69 *https://www.apostolicarchives.com/articles/article/8801925/173917.htm*

70 *https://www.jglm.org/john-g-lake/, https://william-branham.org/site/people/f._f._bosworth*

71 *https://esbs.org/blog/2017/04/04/azusa-street-revival/ https://en.wikipedia.org/wiki/Azusa_Street_Revival*

72 Isaiah 55:10-11

73 Matthew 24:4-5, 11-12

74 Matthew 15:8-9

75 Genesis 11:4

76 Matthew 7:17-18; Luke 6:43

77 *https://www.abarim-publications.com/Meaning/Nimrod.html#. Xmt2AqhKhPY*

78 Genesis 10:8

79 *https://biblehub.com/hebrew/1368.htm*

80 Gill's Exposition of the Entire Bile; Matthew Poole's Commentary *https://biblehub.com/commentaries/genesis/10-9.htm*

81 Hebrews 11:13

82 1 Peter 2:11

83 Genesis 11:4-5 (NKJV)

84 *https://www.abarim-publications.com/Meaning/Babel.html#.X0FPxshKiUk*

85 Genesis 11:9

86 Proverbs 18:10; Judges 9:51

87 Matthew 16:23 (NKJV)

88 John 4:23; 2 Corinthians 5:16

89 1 Corinthians 2:10-16

90 *https://www.ancient.eu/babylon/; https://www.britannica.com/place/Babylon-ancient-city-Mesopotamia-Asia*

[91] *https://www.livescience.com/28701-ancient-babylon-center-of-mesopotamian-civilization.html*

[92] Jeremiah 3:7-11

[93] 2 Kings 18:4

[94] 2 Kings 20:15

[95] 2 Kings 20:17-18; Isaiah 39:6-7

[96] *https://biblehub.com/timeline/*

[97] 1 Corinthians 3:16, 6:19

[98] 2 Corinthians 4:7

[99] 2 Timothy 2:20; 2 Corinthians 7:1; 1 Peter 1:7; Lamentations 4:1-2

[100] 1 Peter 2:9; Revelation 1:6

[101] 2 Corinthians 10:3-5; 2 Timothy 2:3-4

[102] 1 Corinthians 3:9-10

[103] Revelation 3:18

[104] 1 Peter 1:7 (NKJV)

[105] 2 Corinthians 6:10, 8:9; 2 Timothy 2:20-21

[106] Ezekiel 4, 5, 24

[107] Jeremiah 52:6-7

[108] 2 Kings 25:16

[109] Proverbs 9:9; Job 12:12

[110] 1 John 2:14

[111] Hebrews 12:12-13

[112] Luke 14:21; Matthew 22:9

[113] Lamentations 4:1

[114] Jude 22-23; Revelations 2, 3

[115] Daniel 11:31-45; Matthew 24:15; Revelation 17:3

[116] Hebrews 12:14

[117] Revelation 2:6,9,15,20-24, 3:9

[118] Revelation 2:13

[119] Revelation 2:14

[120] Revelation 3:17

[121] 1 Corinthians 13:12

[122] Nehemiah 2:5

[123] Jeremiah 29:10-12

[124] Hebrews 12:22; Revelation 3:12, 21:2,10

[125] Revelation 21:2

[126] Philippians 3:13-14

[127] Haggai 1:4,7-9

[128] 2 Chronicles 7:12-14

[129] Proverbs 21:2

[130] Matthew 7:20

[131] Revelation 2,3

[132] 2 Corinthians 7:1

[133] Romans 6:19

[134] Psalms 133

[135] Isaiah 62:6-7; This scriptural reference shows that God will position people, equip them, and make them responsible partners in the needed work of restoration for His people. We cannot undervalue this work of intercession.

[136] Ephesians 5:27; 2 Corinthians 11:2; Philippians 3:13-14; Joel 1:8

[137] Revelation 2:10

[138] Revelation 19:8; 1 John 3:7

[139] Luke 18:1-8

[140] 1 Kings 18:46

[141] Philippians 2:13

[142] Luke 18:8